CONTEMPORARY ANTISEMITISM

Contemporary Antisemitism

CANADA AND THE WORLD

Edited by
Derek J. Penslar,
Michael R. Marrus,
and
Janice Gross Stein

UNIVERSITY OF TORONTO PRESS
Toronto Buffalo London

© University of Toronto Press Incorporated 2005
Toronto Buffalo London
Printed in Canada

ISBN 0-8020-3931-6

Printed on acid-free paper

Library and Archives Canada Cataloguing in Publication

Contemporary antisemitism : Canada and the world / edited by Derek J.
Penslar, Michael R. Marrus, and Janice Gross Stein.

ISBN 0-8020-3931-6

1. Antisemitism – Canada – Congresses.   2. Antisemitism – Congresses.
I. Penslar, Derek Jonathan   II. Marrus, Michael R., 1941–   III. Stein, Janice

DS145.C66 2005   305.892'4071   C2004-905594-1

University of Toronto Press acknowledges the financial assistance to its publishing
program of the Canada Council for the Arts and the Ontario Arts Council.

University of Toronto Press acknowledges the financial support for its publishing
activities of the Government of Canada through the Book Publishing Industry
Development Program (BPIDP).

Contents

Preface

This volume grew out of a conference, Antisemitism: The Politicization of Prejudice in the Contemporary World, held at the Munk Centre for International Studies at the University of Toronto in February 2003. The conference took place in a heated political climate of international tension and war and was shaped by intense concerns about the revival of forms of prejudice that, many thought, had been consigned to the dustbins of history. Among these, antisemitism, the focus of this volume, is reappearing in new ways and in unexpected strength. However assessed, this resurgence is of deep concern to the academic community and to informed citizens everywhere. And yet, we know too little. Is contemporary antisemitism an eerie echo of the past, or is it driven by new combinations of political, economic, and religious forces? How powerful are the anti-Jewish trends that so many have detected? And how should liberal democratic societies respond? At the University of Toronto, we tried to map the antisemitic terrain, to make important distinctions, and to put various strategies of response into critical perspective.

This volume is the product of intense and fruitful collaboration within the University of Toronto. In particular, the Faculty of Arts and Science, the Faculty of Law, the Jewish Studies Program, the Joint Initiative in German and European Studies, and the School of Graduate Studies provided leadership and financial support. Without their generous help, we could not have mounted the conference. We would especially like to thank President Robert Birgenau, Vice-president and Provost Shirley Neuman, Dean of the Faculty of Law Ronald J. Daniels, Acting Vice-president for Research and International Affairs Carolyn Tuohy, and Vice-president for Advancement Jon Dellandrea, all at the University of Toronto, for their willing assistance and support.

The conference brought together leading academics in Canada and the United States to discuss the contemporary meaning of antisemitism – a question that has, unfortunately, again become pressing for those who have watched events unfold in North America, Europe, and the Middle East at the end of the last century and the beginning of this new one. The two days of discussion and debate that followed were enriched by the breadth of knowledge and the diversity of perspectives of our contributors. Our thanks go to Leonard Dinerstein, Todd M. Endelman, Susan Gross Solomon, Jeffrey Kopstein, Mayo Morgan, Ed Morgan, Richard Simeon, Peter H. Solomon, Jr, Mark Tessler, Robert-Jan Van Pelt, Morton Weinfeld, Lorraine E. Weinrib, Piotr Wróbel, and Steven J. Zipperstein.

Antisemitism is not, of course, only for scholars to analyse. It is a living problem for those engaged in political and legal decision making. Our discussions were enriched by the voices of people who have spent much of their long careers in public life. We thank the Honourable R. Roy McMurtry, Chief Justice of Ontario, and Mr Hershell Ezrin, chairman and chief executive officer of GPC International, for their contribution. We are especially grateful to the Right Honourable Brian Mulroney, a past prime minister of Canada, who opened the conference with an unprecedented and searing examination of Canada's official past. The speech, and the moment, were historic.

As editors, we had an extraordinarily difficult time choosing from among the rich array of contributions. We hope that we have fashioned a volume that is accessible to the interested public, representative of recent research and thinking in North America on antisemitism, and open-minded in its analysis of a long-standing problem. We regret that we could not include all the excellent scholarship that was presented at the conference.

Our thanks go to the following: Ms Mary Lynne Bratti and her assistant, Ms Ilona Milner, at the Munk Centre, who organized the conference with graciousness and skill; Mr Scott Bohaker, who dealt deftly with the conference's challenging technical requirements, from live webcasting to the production of audio compact discs; and Dr Joshua D. Goldstein at the Munk Centre, who helped prepare the manuscript throughout the editorial process. We are grateful, as well, to many colleagues both within and outside the University of Toronto whose scholarly commitment and engagement make them partners in our inquiry and, we hope, critical readers of the pages that follow.

Derek J. Penslar, Director, Jewish Studies Program
Michael R. Marrus, Dean, School of Graduate Studies
Janice Gross Stein, Director, Munk Centre for International Studies

CONTEMPORARY ANTISEMITISM

Introduction

Derek J. Penslar

Antisemitism resists rational explanation and dispassionate inquiry. It is enduring yet protean, featuring undeniable continuities yet also staggering diversity across time and space. Antisemitism not only corrupts those who are seduced by its hateful teachings but can also cloud the judgment of those who strive to combat them. Antisemites and their opponents, whether Jewish or Gentile, regard each other in what is at times an oddly symmetrical fashion: just as the former see the Jew as eternal malefactor, so can the latter perceive antisemitism as embedded into the cultural foundations of Christian and Muslim civilization. The antisemite and his victim might well agree to the presence of a common structure underlying the critique of Judaism and Jews across the ages: the theologically driven antipathies in early Christianity and Islam, the demonization of the Jew as child-killer in medieval Europe, the association in modern times of Jews with both capitalism and communism, and, in our own day, the frequent identification of the Palestinian-Israeli conflict as a cosmic struggle between good and evil. However, whereas for the antisemite the common element is *der ewige Jude* himself, the 'eternal Jew' of Nazi propaganda, his opponent runs the risk of creating a mirror image, the everlasting antisemite, a permanent fixture in a world that will never be free of hatred of the Jews.

It is all too easy for a sane and fair-minded individual to respond to antisemitism through condemnation and dismissal rather than engagement. Because the antisemite's arguments are by their very nature illogical, inaccurate, and indefensible, it might appear a waste of time, even a dangerous legitimization of the antisemite's enterprise, to take the arguments seriously, reconstruct their internal logic, and probe their rhetorical texture. Literary deconstruction, the 'unpacking' of texts, hardly appears warranted when what is being unpacked is a bag of filth. But condemnations of antisemitism based on its existence and harmful effects alone are of only limited benefit. Just as the successful cure of a disease depends on knowledge of its physiological origins, so does an effective response to any social ill require a sound understanding of its causes. Although in the popular imagination antisemitism is often viewed somewhat like a syndrome – a multiplicity of symptoms with a single underlying pathology – on closer examination antisemitism appears quite the opposite, as a symptom with many possible causes.

Scholars have long been aware of this complexity and have produced a vast literature on the history and sociology of antisemitism. When research on antisemitism began in Europe and North America in the late nineteenth century, it was carried out largely by functionaries in Jewish organizations and well-intentioned Gentiles who considered antisemitism to represent a threat to a liberal society and a state based on the rule of law. The first studies of antisemitism were primarily defensive and apologetic, more interested in refutation than social analysis. The pamphlet and the press, manipulated so cleverly by antisemitic publicists, were mobilized by activists eager to serve an embattled minority.[1] Intellectuals were reluctant to engage the subject of antisemitism until the rise of Nazism, the Second World War, and the Holocaust forced them to confront it as a source of the collapse of Western civilization. During the Second World War, Theodor Adorno and other German-Jewish émigré intellectuals took part in the Berkeley Project on the Nature and Extent of Antisemitism, from which emerged the mammoth volume *The Authoritarian Personality*, published in 1950. As the book's title suggests, antisemitism was placed within a broad framework of psychological and sociological dysfunction that promoted authoritarian and prejudiced behaviour of various types. Hannah Arendt's *The Origins of Totalitarianism*, published in the same year as *The Authoritarian Personality*, devotes its first section to antisemitism, considering it, along with imperialism, chauvinism, and the collapse of stable class structures, to be one component of several behind the development of the Nazi and Stalinist states.[2] Along a parallel track with the work of Arendt, Adorno, and other German-Jewish émigré intellectuals reacting to the Holocaust, American social scientists, repelled by segregation against blacks, pioneered comparative research in antisemitism and racism as forms of intergroup prejudice. In books such as Gordon Willard Allport's *The Nature of Prejudice* (1954), bigotry and prejudice are considered to be harmful, yet ameliorable, aberrations from the liberal order.[3]

Antisemitism's centrality in the sociology of prejudice began to be questioned in the 1960s, however, as discriminatory barriers against North American Jews fell far more quickly than those against blacks. In the United States, while Jews enjoyed unprecedented social mobility and access to positions in the federal government, Ivy League universities, and prestigious hospitals, blacks raged against their stagnating and ghettoized conditions. A host of other factors – American involvement in the Vietnam War, Israel's crushing victory in the 1967 war and subsequent territorial expansion, and a flourishing of anticolonial movements throughout the world – led in the West to a radicalization of academic politics and the rise to prominence of ethnic and postcolonial studies in which the issue of antisemitism was pushed to the periphery. Tellingly, from the late 1960s, in the academic lexicon the word 'prejudice' was replaced by 'racism': the former refers to an act of prejudgment of an individual's character based on assumptions about the group (religious, ethnic, national, or racial) with which (s)he claims affiliation, whereas the latter transforms race into a prism through which all cognition and self-awareness is refracted. Since Jews are, by and large, considered 'white' – not just in the sense of pigmentation but, more broadly, in their class and cultural milieus – they do not easily fit into what has become the dominant academic framework for the study of intergroup antipathy. To be sure, from the 1960s to our own day, a vast body of scholarship on the history of antisemitism has been produced, but this literature treats antisemitism as a historical, not a living, phenomenon, and its producers are for the most part scholars in Jewish studies and theologians who, however worthy their projects, speak mainly to each other and to like-minded members of the educated public and exert little impact on academia as a whole.[4]

Throughout much of the postwar period, the distancing of antisemitism from the academic radar screen has appeared to be justified by broader social trends. For more than half a century after 1945, levels of antisemitism in North America steadily declined. In the United States, in 1964 29 per cent of Americans believed that Jews held 'too much power'; by 1998 the figure had dropped to 12 per cent, and in 2000 the Democratic candidate for the presidency, Al Gore, saw only benefit in the path-breaking choice of a Jew, Joseph Lieberman, as his running mate. In North America antisemitic incidents occurred regularly, but they were the work of a minuscule minority. Rarely involving personal assaults, they took the form of vandalism, as in the spate of attacks against synagogues and Jewish cemeteries in 1960, or, more frequently, threatening and hateful speech, which from the 1970s onward was often associated with Holocaust denial. Antisemitism took a more violent turn in Europe, largely because of a greater vulnerability to terrorist activity growing out of the Arab-Israeli conflict. But even in Europe, outside of the Soviet Union and its satellites, classic antisemitism was no longer socially acceptable and was opposed by the political elites.

In the last three years, however, the stability of the postwar environment has been threatened. Since 2000 there has been an alarming increase of hate crimes directed against Jews and Jewish spaces (synagogues, schools, cemeteries) throughout the world. Several incidents related to the Middle East – the onset of the second Palestinian uprising in September 2000; the destruction a year later of the World Trade Center by terrorists from Saudi Arabia, Egypt, the United Arab Emirates, and Lebanon; and the Israeli reoccupation of the West Bank in April of 2002 – served as proximate causes for attacks against Jews in places as far-flung as Los Angeles and London, Marseilles and Mombasa. In Europe, antisemitism has been stimulated by not only external factors but also internal ones, such as anti-immigrant sentiment in the West and aggressive nationalism in East European lands recently freed from the Iron Curtain.

Few academics in North America, and fewer still in Europe, have addressed the question of a revived or intensified antisemitism in the post-9/11 world. As in previous decades in the postwar era, antisemitism is believed to be a marginal phenomenon that pales in comparison with racism and misogyny, and anti-Jewish hate crimes, although deeply regrettable, are usually conceived as manifestations of unresolved ethnic conflicts (as in France, where disaffected North Africans are responsible for most antisemitic incidents) or as a spillover from the Arab-Israeli conflict, whose political and territorial dimensions are thought to remove it from the framework of classic antisemitism. Threats to global stability caused by unequal relations of power and wealth between the West (particularly the United States) and the developing world or by the politicization of Islam are more likely to attract sustained scholarly attention than the situation of the Jews.

As was the case a century ago, when Jewish activists assumed the burden of confronting antisemitism, so today critical discourse on recent outbursts of antisemitism has been dominated by leaders of Jewish organizations and defenders of Jewish causes. Recent works by the political activist Phyllis Chesler, Harvard law professor Alan Dershowitz, and Abraham Foxman of the B'nai Brith's Anti-Defamation League argue that current manifestations of antisemitism, including those spawned by the Arab-Israeli conflict, are deeply rooted in earlier forms of Jew-hatred and that contemporary antisemitism presents a grave threat to the well-being of Jews worldwide.[5] These books make a number of valid claims, but by their very nature, as apologetic and polemical works, they leave little room for nuance, disinterested analysis, or a multiplicity of perspectives.

Thus the need for this book, which seeks not merely to describe antisemitism in our own day but to interrogate it; to depict how, where, and why it flourishes; to demonstrate its multiplicity of forms and causes, its links and breaks with the past; and, based on all this information, to suggest how it can be addressed. It brings together pronunciations by public figures and the ruminations of scholars. The essays gathered here represent multiple points of view. Some support, albeit in a more nuanced fashion, Chesler's and Foxman's claim that contemporary antisemitism is of a piece with its earlier manifestations and that antisemitism lies at the heart of most of the critical public discourse on Israel. Other essays stress rupture more than continuity, and describe public sensibility about the Arab-Israeli conflict as moulded by not only venerable forms of Jew-hatred but also contemporary expressions of political and ethnic animosity. Just as the articles in this volume do not offer a monolithic explanation for the sources and nature of contemporary antisemitism, neither do they agree about the level of threat it presents or its future course.

The essays progress from the terrain most familiar to the reader – contemporary Canada – to the Western world as a whole, and thence to the Middle East, the most important source of, or at least justification for, antisemitism today. This volume is unusual in that it combines the voices of scholars with those of political and judicial leaders (who have also, as a whole, been slow or unwilling to speak out firmly against recent anti-Jewish hate crimes). Part I offers two moving essays by Canadian leaders. It begins with an address by former Prime Minister Brian Mulroney, who combines an erudite analysis of the sources of modern antisemitism with an unsparing critique of Canada's chequered historical record in confronting antisemitism both at home and abroad. Whereas Mulroney focuses on the role of elected officials in protecting our open society, R. Roy McMurtry, Chief Justice of Ontario, analyses the role of the Canadian judicial system in restraining antisemitic activity and expression.

The book's second and major component is a series of essays by scholars of antisemitism throughout the globe. It begins with a paper by sociologist Morton Weinfeld, who provides the context for Mulroney's and McMurtry's remarks by employing demographic and survey data to offer a valuable comparison between antisemitism and other forms of group hatred in contemporary Canada and by observing the limits as well as the extent of antisemitism in Canadian society. The essays that follow broaden the focus to include the United States and Europe. Two scholars of modern Jewish history, Steven Zipperstein and Todd Endelman, demonstrate multiple areas of continuity and rupture between contemporary and previous forms of antisemitism. The essays differ in focus and tenor. Endelman focuses on the sources of antisemitism in contemporary Europe and notes the role that hostility to Israel plays therein. Zipperstein's approach is more expansive, ranging across North America and Europe and intertwining the definition and analysis of antisemitism with questions of Jewish perceptions thereof. Derek Penslar's essay completes the book's historical offerings, building a conceptual bridge between European antisemitism and Arab anti-Zionism throughout the twentieth century. In the book's final essay, political scientist Mark Tessler returns the reader's focus back to the present, here offering fascinating public-opinion data that challenge much of the conventional wisdom about the nature of Arab antisemitism and the role of politicized Islam in fomenting it.

Although three of the seven essays in this volume are the work of historians, the focus of the book is contemporary. Historical analysis is driven not by a thirst for abstract knowledge but by the belief that, consciously or not, historical thinking underlies our social consciousness and the way we make sense out of current affairs. In politics, as in art, framing and perspective are inextricably linked. If, for example, in the collective memory antisemitism is viewed as eternal and fundamentally unchanging, then attitudes towards the present situation will be far different than if it is seen as a manifestation of specific historical circumstance, more as a symptom than a syndrome. The question of appropriate response – fatalism, passivity, activism, and if the last, what sort of activism – can be answered only through an understanding of the nature of antisemitism in a particular time and place.

The problem of how one frames, and thus perceives, antisemitic discourse, policy, or acts of violence is literally an ancient one. In 38 CE, the city of Alexandria was engulfed by anti-Jewish riots fuelled by Egyptian resentment against Roman rule and the favourable political status of Jews in the city. Some of the Roman Empire's greatest figures – Cicero, Tacitus, Juvenal – decried Judaism as a superstitious and intolerant religion and Jews as clannish and disloyal. Were these incidents and expressions 'antisemitic' – that is, motivated by an irrational yet coherently structured matrix of anti-Jewish sensibilities? If so, were they representative of Gentile feelings about Jews in pagan antiquity, or did they represent the exception to the rule? (After all, Jewish life flourished for more than four centuries in ancient Alexandria, and under the Roman Empire Judaism was a widely popular, proselytizing religion.)

Anti-Jewish rhetoric alone provides poor evidence about the overall viability of Jewish communities across time and space. After the Christianization of the Roman Empire in the fourth century CE, Jews were frequently subject to discriminatory legislation, and a picture of Jewish life in early Christendom derived from those texts alone would be grim indeed. Yet throughout the early centuries of Christianity, close social contacts between Jews and Gentiles continued, much to the consternation of the Church Fathers, whose vicious diatribes against the Jews were at least in part the product of frustration that Christians were socializing with Jews and visiting synagogues. In certain times and places (e.g., Charlemagne's empire), Jews enjoyed greater economic and legal liberties than many Christians. One encounters a similar set of contradictions when examining the fate of Jews in the founding period of Islam. On the one hand, Muslim foundational texts are replete with anti-Jewish imagery; yet on the other, Jews flourished in medieval Islam as nowhere else since the heyday of pagan antiquity.

As is well known, in the late Middle Ages and early modern period Jews in Europe were frequently the targets of mob justice, government-sponsored torture and execution, and expulsion. Once again, however, the issue of framing is crucial. As the historian David Niremberg has observed in a study of Jewish life in medieval Christian Spain, mob action against Jews most often took the form of restrained and ritualized displays of superiority: the shouting of epithets, the throwing of stones at the doors to Jewish homes.[6] This is not to minimize the extent of antisemitism, but in an environment suffused with group hatreds, blood feuds, and honour killings, the position of Jews was not necessarily more precarious than that of many others. In the great Jewish civilization that flourished in early modern Poland and Lithuania, Catholic antisemitism did not, in and of itself, impinge upon the liberties of a population that, unlike the Christian peasantry, experienced considerable freedom of movement and occupation. Even in the nineteenth-century Russian Empire, home to state-sponsored antisemitism and, towards the end of the century, the site of numerous bloody pogroms, Jews were, in virtually every way, better off than the masses of serfs.

Comparative approaches to the study of antisemitism are threatened with paralysis as they approach the subject of the Holocaust. The words 'however,' 'on the other hand,' and 'in comparison with others' appear to lose their credibility when confronted by the greatest tragedy in the history of the Jewish people. In fact, comparative studies of the Holocaust and other genocides are highly valuable, partly in their explication of the common societal and technological forces that make modern genocide possible, but also in their highlighting of the unique qualities of the Nazi genocide. More relevant to the purview of this volume, however, is the necessity not to conceive of Jewish history in a deterministic, teleological manner, in which the Holocaust becomes a diabolical telos to which the diaspora Jewish experience inexorably led. The editors would stress the contingent qualities of historical development, which, although explicable in terms of broad socio-economic or collective-psychological forces, is not beholden to them. History has many futures. It is precisely this way of thinking that illustrates the magnitude of the horror of the Holocaust: modern Jewish history did not have to lead to Auschwitz because Auschwitz did not have to be built.

The Nazis' murderous antisemitism had nothing to do with real Jews; rather, it was a mixture of irrational phobias and fantasies. The Nazis drew upon both traditional Christian Jew-hatred and modern political antisemitism. The latter, which emerged in the 1880s, presented Jew-hatred as a systematic ideology, an 'ism,' a secular world view on par with the great competing ideologies of the era, liberalism and socialism. Political antisemitism identified the Jews as responsible for all the anxiety-provoking social forces that characterized modernity: ruthless capitalism, revolutionary communism, avant-garde artistic modernism. Modern antisemitism was, thus, far more than yet another form of bigotry or xenophobia. It was, as the historian Shulamit Volkov has put it, a 'cultural code,' a signifier of social protest by individuals unwilling or unable to confront the real sources of their anxiety and despair.[7] As some of the essays in this volume point out, there are lines of continuity between the old antisemitism and the new in the role that anti-Jewish sentiment plays in the antiglobalization movement and the extent to which Israel is considered by many people the world over to be the prime source of international instability. But along with the continuities come differences as well – essential ones – for the Arab-Israeli conflict, a dispute involving an empowered Jewish state, does introduce heretofore unknown factors into the antisemitic equation. Moreover, in North America and Europe today antisemitism is not state-sponsored or sanctioned. It is, for the most part, socially unacceptable, and its flare-ups are minuscule in comparison with the daily humiliations and limitations with which Jews had to contend even in the most enlightened Western countries from the late nineteenth through the mid-twentieth centuries.

Underlying the public debate in Canada today about antisemitism are profound, yet usually unconscious, differences in approach to the relationship between the present and the past. Many individuals operate under the assumption that change over time is more epiphenomenal than substantive, that the course of history resembles, if not a circle, then a fractal, a geometric form that may have the most variegated appearance but any part of which embodies the fundamental mathematical structure of the whole. According to this world view, the widely varying contexts in which antisemitism has flourished over the ages are merely a superstructure constructed upon a base of Judeophobia that has been ingrained into Christian and Muslim civilization since their inception and that lives on today, albeit in an often secularized form. The editors of this volume acknowledge that there is some truth to this perspective, for certain antisemitic motifs, like viruses, are transmitted across vast distances of time and space, periodically mutating into ever more lethal forms.

Yet we would like readers to consider an alternative view, one that conceives of history as filled with ruptures as well as continuities, with quantum changes in perception and definition. Upon closer view, what Lord Acton called the seamless web of history actually resembles a vast jigsaw puzzle, a coherent whole composed of discrete shapes that are joined tightly together, yet each with its own distinct features and qualities. The travails experienced by Jews in the world of 2003 are grave, but they are not identical to those suffered in 1933, or 1648, or any other era in history. Antisemitism in the early twenty-first century represents a real threat, to the well-being not only of Jews but also of the societies in which they live, and it is the editors' hope that readers of this book will join with Mr Mulroney and Justice McMurtry in vowing to combat it. We ask, though, that the battle be conducted with awareness of the context in which antisemitism has flourished anew, sensitivity to the connections between antisemitism and other forms of politicized prejudice, a sage combination of instruments of persuasion and coercion, and an appreciation of the flexibility and resilience of Canada's open society.

NOTES

1 Much of this research was produced by Jewish activists and Gentile opponents of antisemitism in Imperial Germany. For an overview of this literature, see Ismar Schorsch, *Jewish Reactions to Antisemitism in Germany, 1870–1914* (New York: Columbia University Press, 1972).

2 Theodor Adorno, Else Frenkel-Brunswik, Daniel J. Levinson, and R. Nevitt Sanford, *The Authoritarian Personality* (New York: Harper and Row, 1950); Hannah Arendt, *The Origins of Totalitarianism* (New York: Harcourt Brace Jovanovich, 1951). Jean-Paul Sartre's long essay *Antisemite and Jew* (1946) may in some ways be considered of a piece with this first wave of intellectual engagement with antisemitism, although its intent is less the diagnosis of social pathology than an exploration of individual existential panic.

3 Gordon Willard, *The Nature of Prejudice* (Cambridge, MA: Addison-Wesley, 1954).

4 The historiography on antisemitism is immense and would fill a book-length bibliography. The first major overview was Léon Poliakov, *The History of Antisemitism*, IV, v (Oxford: Littman Library, 1985) (French original, 1966–77). More recent synthetic accounts include Jacob Katz, *From Prejudice to Destruction: Antisemitism, 1700–1933* (Cambridge, MA: Harvard University Press, 1980); Robert Wistrich, *Antisemitism: The Longest Hatred* (New York: Pantheon, 1991); Albert S. Lindemann, *Esau's Tears: Modern Anti-Semitism and the Rise of the Jews* (Cambridge: Cambridge University Press, 1997); and Marvin Perry and Frederick M. Schweitzer, *Antisemitism: Myth and Hate from Antiquity to the Present* (New York: Palgrave Macmillan, 2002).

5 Phyllis Chesler, *The New Anti-Semitism: The Current Crisis and What We Must Do*

about It (Hoboken, NJ: John Wiley and Sons, 2003); Alan Dershowitz, *The Case for Israel* (Hoboken, NJ: John Wiley and Sons, 2003); Abraham Foxman, *Never Again? The Threat of the New Antisemitism* (New York: HarperCollins, 2003).

6 David Niremberg, *Communities of Violence* (Princeton: Princeton University Press, 1997).

7 Shulamit Volkov, 'Antisemitism as a Cultural Code,' *Leo Baeck Institute Year Book XXIII* (1978): 25–45.

PART I

Canadian Leaders on Antisemitism

Chapter 1

Antisemitism: An Enduring Reality

THE RIGHT HONOURABLE BRIAN MULRONEY

This volume begins with a unique and historic document. The Right Honourable Brian Mulroney, Prime Minister of Canada between 1984 and 1993, offers a powerful condemnation of antisemitism that spares neither the Roman Catholic Church in which he was raised nor Canadian society, which, throughout the first half of the twentieth century, was deeply stained by prejudice against Jews. Reminding us of Canada's shameful immigration policies towards Jews during the 1930s and 1940s, and of ongoing manifestations of antisemitism in our own era, Mulroney urges Canadians never to sink into complacency or to allow ideals of Canadian diversity and toleration to mask the hatreds that abide among us.

* * *

I was born in Baie Comeau, Quebec, then a small town on the St Lawrence River, in 1939, the year the Nazis marched and the Allies responded.

My only recollections of the war are scenes of my dad – then a father of three young children – marching proudly up Champlain Street with fellow militia members, getting ready to serve if called. And I can still remember children's whispers of German submarines lurking off our shores and my electrician father at dinner telling his family of the horrors of Hitler and why he had to be crushed if civilization were to be saved. My sisters and I listened attentively but understood very little of the unspeakable reality he sought to describe.

There were no Jews in Baie Comeau. Just plain old Catholics and Protestants, French and English, living together in a degree of serenity that would, I am sure, surprise some future Quebec leaders.

I met my first Jew in Chatham, New Brunswick, in 1955 when I attended St Thomas High School. His name was Bobby Jacobson, a local haberdasher and a respected member of the Miramichi community. I liked him at our first encounter.

I moved on to university in Nova Scotia and had friendly but intermittent relationships with some members of the Jewish community there, but it was not until I entered law school at Université Laval in Quebec City in 1960 that I really came to know Jews for the first time. I was by then twenty years of age.

I had two Jewish classmates there, Michael Kastner and Israel (Sonny) Mass, one from a wealthy family and one working class like me. They were both intelligent, interesting, pleasant classmates. We became friends and remain so to this day. I learned about the tiny but impressive Jewish community there but little of its history and challenges in Canada.

It was when I graduated and moved to Montreal to practise law in 1964 – almost forty years ago – that I first came into contact with a large Jewish community, which, as it turned out, ignited my interest in and support of the Jews and Israel.

By this time, of course, the horrors of the Holocaust and the systematic persecution of Jews were well known and fully documented. Why, I asked myself, would such evil be visited upon anyone, including, and specifically, the families of this large and vibrant community I was getting to know for the first time?

The Jews of Montreal were, in my judgment, remarkable. Families were close, values were taught, education was revered, work was honoured, and success was expected; these principles had spawned over the decades an extraordinary community of teachers, doctors, lawyers, writers, and business leaders.

How could it be, I often wondered, that the progenitors of such a law-abiding and productive group that was demonstrably making such a powerful contribution to the economic, cultural, and political life of Montreal and Canada were reviled over centuries and systematically murdered in a six-year period, beginning in the year of my birth? Thus began my first serious reflections on and encounters with antisemitism.

Following the Holocaust, the cry of 'Never again' became both affirmation and promise. We expected that humanity would forswear antisemitism forever. The founding of the State of Israel in 1948 reinforced this hope. Unfortunately, today, Jewish communities and the world's only Jewish state globally confront this re-emergent evil.

This latest antisemitism did not surface suddenly, in a vacuum. Rather than constituting a new phenomenon, it forms part of a historical continuum that was only briefly interrupted, if at all, in the years immediately following the Second World War. Instead of declaring 'Never again,' we find ourselves painfully asking where did it all come from, what makes it so resistant to suppression, and will it ever end?

Antisemitism, it has to be said, has nothing to do with Semites and everything to do with Jews. The term, as you well know, was first used in the nineteenth century. It was another one of those ideological 'isms' so current then. Intended to give a name to Jew-hatred as a political platform, it subsequently came to encapsulate the manifestation of Judeophobia throughout history.

It all begins, I think, in that chronological transitional period from BC to AD. It was a time of great religious ferment, with a variety of faiths vying for the attention of the seekers. This choice-filled free market came abruptly to a halt in 70 AD. Canadian scholar Donald Akenson, of Queen's University, in his *Surpassing Wonder: The Invention of the Bible and the Talmuds*,[1] demonstrates that the destruction by the Romans of Jerusalem's Second Jewish Temple was the pivotal event of that era. Only Christianity and Judaism, he tells us, survived the catastrophe because they were the two religions able to overcome it intellectually and to develop pragmatic strategies for carrying on.

Originally, the people who followed Jesus, it would be fair to say, considered themselves Jews. Once a Christian Church quickly evolved, however, recognizing Christ as the Messiah and as the incarnation of God on earth, the divisions between Judaism and Christianity were crystallized.

The younger religion proceeded to differentiate and disassociate itself from its antecedent. In fact, the Church took up an antagonistic position towards Judaism and its practitioners. This is reflected in the Gospel accounts and the writings of the early Church Fathers, which would be elaborated upon and exacerbated in the centuries to follow.

Jews, first and foremost, were branded with the most devastating of charges – Deicide. They were accused, furthermore, of the stubborn refusal to accept Christ's Godhead and His sacrifice, which was all the more damning because they were of His very blood. They were pictured as consumed with a detestation of Christianity and as defilers of its rituals and symbols. They were the agents of Satan and the future allies if not the progenitors of Antichrist. Their ultimate aim was to destroy the one true faith.

We can well imagine, as a result, how ordinary men and women would have felt about Jews. Individuals in the medieval world were overcome by fear, fear of a world where so little was understood and so much left unexplained. Demons lurked everywhere, mostly in the shadows, unseen and therefore beyond retribution.

There was, however, one viable demon against whom one could retaliate – the Jew. It was the Jew who poisoned the wells and was responsible for the Black Death. The disappearance of children, in what has become known as the 'Blood libel,' was readily and falsely blamed on alleged Jewish murderers who required the blood of Christian children for their nefarious rituals.

Over the centuries, the venomous ideological superstructure and the paranoid substructure exacted a very high price in Jewish blood and infected countless Christians with the soul-devouring virus of Jew-hatred. Nonetheless, until the early modern period, theoretically at least, it was only the Jew's religion that authorities found objectionable.

Those Jews who converted were legally on a par with their fellow Christians, free to exercise any economic activity and to compete for all offices of church and state. While this might have been the official view, at the popular level the constant and protracted anti-Jewish campaign could not but have transformed religious animosity into racial hatred.

The founding of the Inquisition in fifteenth-century Spain fully effected the transition from religious to racial antisemitism. The issue in Christian-Jewish relations was no longer God but genes.

Ferdinand and Isabella, following the practice of other European monarchs, expelled their Jews in 1492. At the same time they subjected the converted Jews, or 'new Christians' as they came to be called (even if they had been Christian for a number of generations), to many of the disabilities that previously had been imposed on Jews as an incentive for conversion. The Inquisition, furthermore, was to keep an intensely watchful eye on them until the early nineteenth century, to immunize blood and faith from contamination.

The Nazis, with their emphasis on racial and ideological purity, were the natural inheritors of those who, for two millennia, have been centrally motivated by antisemitism. Nothing captures better the antisemite's single-mindedness than Ron Rosenbaum's account, in his book *Explaining Hitler,* of the Führer, just prior to his suicide, as the Third Reich lay in ruins, calling on Germans 'still above all else never to cease from the struggle against the Jews, the eternal poisoners of the world.'[2]

Who would have imagined that this call, virtually from the grave, would once again be heeded, almost sixty years after the defeat of Nazism, at the beginning of the twenty-first century and the second millennium? Observers in Israel, Europe, North America, and elsewhere have described this 'new' antisemitism as the worst concentrated outbreak since the end of the Second World War.

I think there have been genuinely impressive improvements in the status of Jews in modern society as well as their ungrudging acceptance in leadership positions that affect all facets of our lives. But as one grappling with what accounts for antisemitism's persistence, I am distressed by its incomprehensible resilience. Classical antisemites portrayed the Jewish people as an alien and evil force responsible for mankind's ills and engaged in a conspiracy either to undermine Christian civilization or, more recently, to conquer the world. Their ultimate aim was to expel Jews from the human family.

Contemporary antisemitism, without changing its stripes, has added the State of Israel to its list of targets. The current goal is to deny the Jewish state its rightful place among the community of nations. For Islamic and Arab extremists and others of this ilk who have, for example, domesticated Europe's antisemitic themes, with their unholy allies on the extreme right and the radical left, Israel has in effect become the new Jew.

Canadians talk proudly of our tolerance and fair-mindedness. Often a tone of moral superiority insinuates itself into our national discourse. But these virtues are of fairly recent vintage. The truth is, we have little to be smug about. For instance, in 1933, Toronto witnessed the Christie Pits riot when local antisemites terrorized a Jewish baseball team in a street battle that went on all night.[3]

The next year, in Montreal, all the interns at Hospital Nôtre-Dame went on strike to protest the hiring of a Jew as their colleague. The Jew in question, one Samuel Rabinovitch, had graduated first in his class at l'Université de Montréal but was forced to resign after a few days because, as *Le Devoir* reported, Catholic patients would find it 'repugnant' to be treated or touched by a Jewish doctor.[4]

In 1938, the Canadian Jewish Congress decided not to publish a study of the status of Jews in English Canada because the findings were so profoundly unsettling.[5]

But overt antisemitism and an abject failure to appreciate its ultimate consequences if unchecked were not parochial considerations, nor were they limited to minor players in Canadian society.

On 10 February 1937, Canada's Prime Minister Mackenzie King records in his diary a friendly chance encounter he had had the previous Monday night with an elderly man on Wilbrod Street in Ottawa.

The man, a Russian immigrant called Mr Cohen, tells the Prime Minister that he had built a furniture and clothing business on Rideau and Banks Streets, that he had three sons and a daughter, and that he had divided all he possessed among them and was now living in retirement with his daughter. In other words, a true Canadian success story.

The Prime Minister listened to Mr Cohen thoughtfully, treated him kindly, and then recorded the following in his diary: 'The only unfortunate part of the whole story is that the Jews having acquired foothold of Sandy Hill, it will not be long before this part of Ottawa will become more or less possessed by them. I should not be surprised if, some time later, Laurier House was left as about the only residence not occupied by Jews in this part of the city.'[6]

A few months later, Prime Minister King visited Germany to meet Chancellor Adolf Hitler. King recorded the following impressions of that meeting:

He [Hitler] smiled very pleasantly and indeed had a sort of appealing and affectionate look in his eyes. My sizing up of the man as I sat and talked with him was that he is really one who truly loves his fellow-men ...

His face is much more pre-possessing than his pictures would give the impression of. It is not that of a fiery over-strained nature but of a calm, passive man deeply and thoughtfully in earnest. His skin was smooth. His face did not present lines of fatigue or weariness. His eyes impressed me most of all. There was a liquid quality about them which indicates keen perception and profound sympathy ... [O]ne could see, how particularly humble folk would come to have profound love for the man ...

As I talked with him I could not but think of Joan of Arc. He is distinctly a mystic.[7]

The following day, our prime minister had lunch in Berlin with the Nazi foreign minister, von Neurath, who delivered himself of some interesting opinions:

He admitted that they [the Nazis] had taken some pretty rough steps in cleaning up the situation, but the truth was the country was going to pieces at the time Hitler took hold. He said to me that I would have loathed living in Berlin with the Jews, and the way in which they had increased their numbers in the city, and were taking possession of its more important part. He said there was no pleasure in going to a theatre which was filled with them. Many of them were very coarse and vulgar and assertive. They were getting control of all the business, the finance, and had really taken advantage of the necessity of the people. It was necessary to get them out to have the Germans really control their own city and affairs. He told me I would have been surprised at the extent to which life and morale had become demoralized; that Hitler had set his face against all that kind of thing, and had tried to inspire desire for a good life in the minds of young people.[8]

And how did Canada's prime minister react to these diabolically racist and extremely ominous comments by one of the most powerful leaders of the Third Reich? Mackenzie King wrote, 'I left him feeling that I had met a man whose confidence I would continue to enjoy through the rest of my days.'[9] A day later he records, 'After returning to the hotel, I wrote a letter of some length by hand to von Neurath whom I like exceedingly. He is, if there ever was one, a genuinely kind, good man.'[10]

The prime minister sets both the agenda and the tone in Ottawa. Is it any wonder, then, that Canada was slammed shut to Jewish immigrants before and during the war and, when asked how many Jews would be allowed into Canada after the war, a senior immigration official famously replied, 'None is too many'?[11] Most regrettably, the Government of Canada even refused entry to a ship called the *St Louis*, bearing a shipload of Jews desperate for Canada to admit them, but who instead sailed back to Europe on a voyage of the damned.

This was a moment when Canada's heritage and promise were betrayed. Canada's conduct was absolutely disgraceful, and I continue to be deeply troubled by the insouciance of our federal government confronted by such a stark and transparent moral challenge. To this day, I cannot watch footage of the faces of Jewish mothers, fathers, and children consigned to the gas chambers in German concentration camps without, as a Canadian, feeling a great sense of sorrow, loss, and guilt.

The Government of Canada ignored not only the plight of the Jews but also the protests of the Canadian people and the pleading of the press. A prominent Montrealer, William Birks, called the government's closed-door policy 'narrow, bigoted and short sighted.' Socialist leader J.S. Woodsworth said he felt 'helpless and ashamed' as a Canadian. The *Toronto Star* and the *Winnipeg Free Press* condemned Ottawa's 'cowardly policy.'[12]

Why was nothing done? Because of political expediency; because the Prime Minister had a visceral distrust of Jews and was afraid he could not carry his cabinet on an open-door policy, which in government circles was very unpopular.

But prime ministers are not chosen to seek popularity. They are elected to provide leadership. Prime ministers are supposed to tell Canadians not what they want *to hear* but what they have *to know*. And what they have to know is a quotation from the Book of Proverbs inscribed on the Peace Tower in Ottawa: 'Where there is no vision, the people perish.' Above all, it is the prime minister's responsibility to lead on the great moral issues of the day. Because of Ottawa's abdication of moral leadership, countless Jews perished in Hitler's death camps and we as a country were deprived of them, their children, and the glory of their lives. Antisemitism is born in ignorance and nurtured in envy. It is the stepchild of delusion and evil.

The ongoing success of Canada's Jewish community is consequently often misunderstood, misrepresented, and misreported. The rise in the number of attacks on Jews and Jewish institutions in Canada and the pathetic but startling ravings of David Ahenakew testify to the intractability of the problem and the constant need for vigilance, consistency, and strength in dealing with the entire sweep of antisemitism. John F. Kennedy once remarked, in words he attributed to Dante, that 'the hottest places in hell are reserved for those who in a period of moral crisis maintain their neutrality.'[13] In fact, ambivalence on an issue of such importance is for the cowardly, which is why each of us must stand up and be counted, and why our elected leaders cannot duck or dodge.

Prime ministers are not exempt from this rule and, because I served in that office for almost nine years, let me briefly recount some personal experiences.

In 1967, while a very young lawyer, I made my first (modest) contribution through Neil Phillips, QC, to the defence of Israel. It was a moment of extreme peril for Israel, and I simply wanted to show my support.

In 1976, at a Quebec Economic Summit in La Malbaie chaired by Premier Lévesque, I was astonished to hear Yvon Charbonneau, then president of La Corporation des Enseignants du Quebec (now an MP from Montreal) denounce Sam Steinberg and other Montreal Jewish leaders in what I considered a decidedly racist manner. I was then executive vice-president of Iron Ore of Canada, and in the absence of a more authoritative representative I demanded the microphone and denounced Charbonneau and his views on the spot.

When the federal government in 1984 invited the PLO United Nations representative to be heard in Parliament before a committee (at a time when the PLO was officially known as a terrorist organization), as leader of the Opposition I summoned the Israeli ambassador from his sick bed to my office in the Centre Block so that we could jointly excoriate both the government and the PLO.

Early in my first term as prime minister, my government appointed the Deschênes Commission of Inquiry on Nazi war criminals who had escaped to Canada, because, as I said then, 'our citizenship shall not be dishonoured by those who preach hatred,' and that 'Canada shall never become a safe haven for such persons.' The Deschênes Commission's work was controversial and painful for some communities infiltrated by war criminals, communities of rock-solid Canadians who had heroically served our country in war and steadfastly built it in peace. Many wondered why we were so determined to dredge up this painful episode from our past.

In fact, much more could have been achieved had such a commission been appointed some decades earlier when the evidence was fresher and the suspects much younger. But Ottawa had refused to act. I insisted that, in any event, the government should proceed with this major initiative because it was simply the right thing to do for the Holocaust survivors, for the dignity of the Jewish community, and for the honour of Canada.

I appointed Jews to my Cabinet and to the highest reaches of the public service and judiciary.

I appointed three Jews in succession – Stanley Hartt, Norman Spector, and Hugh Segal – as chief of staff to the prime minister, perhaps the most sensitive and influential unelected position in Ottawa.

I appointed Norman Spector as Canada's first Jewish ambassador to Israel, smashing in the process the odious myth of dual loyalties that had prevented Jews from serving in that position for forty years.

I invited Chaim Herzog to make an official state visit to Canada, the first by a President of Israel since the founding of the Jewish state. On 27 June 1989, I had the high honour of introducing President Herzog as he spoke to a joint session of the House of Commons and Senate.

Senator David Croll was an outstanding member of the Jewish community from Ontario, elected to Parliament as a Liberal in 1945. He was widely considered Cabinet material who never made Cabinet for no apparent reason at the time other than his Jewishness. I decided to elevate this remarkable Canadian to the Privy Council on his ninetienth birthday so that he would, finally, be recognized as a member of the Queen's Privy Council for Canada.

My own view of Canada's foreign policy in the Middle East was articulated as leader of the Opposition when I said that Canada under my government would treat fairly with the moderate nations in the region, such as Jordan under the late great King Hussein, but that, first and foremost, Canada would make an 'unshakable commitment' to the integrity and well-being of Israel. And for nine years we did precisely that, faithfully supporting Israel at home and around the world. As prime minister, I saw to that personally.

We decided to commit Canada to participate in the Gulf War to liberate Kuwait from the Iraqis in 1991. There were many reasons why we undertook that action: concern for the territorial integrity of a friendly country and our own collective security, including, as well, the security of Israel. I believe history will record we did the right thing.

I have always believed that considerations of its internal security are for Israel, and Israel alone, to determine. In 1993, as Canada's prime minister I was the first foreign leader invited to meet with President Clinton, and we later gave a joint news conference on the South Lawn of the White House, where we were asked about the prospects for the peace process. Here is what I said then: 'I'm always very concerned when people start to lecture Israel on the manner in which it looks after its own internal security, because for very important historical reasons, Israel is of course better qualified than most to make determinations about its own well-being.' I believe that to be true today.

Canada is a marvellous country that has provided sanctuary and opportunity to millions. But our history has not been untroubled in this regard. Many groups of immigrants to Canada have suffered injustice and discrimination. From the Japanese to the Ukrainians to the Irish to the Italians to the Chinese, and so many others, the streets of Canada turned out not to be paved with gold, and the voyage to Canadian citizenship was often marked by sadness and despair.

But the story of the Jews remains markedly different. The Holocaust saw to that. Accordingly, these decisions and gestures I have recounted – and many more by other leaders of all political parties – are important both substantively and symbolically. I believe they represent in some measure how a prime minister should act, because they send out signals to the nation and the world of where Canada stands on this extremely vital question. When I ceased being prime minister, I maintained that attitude, publicly denouncing those, from the United Nations to the Canadian government to foreign governments and organizations, who showed hostility or malice to Israel or the Jews.

And why is it important that we all continue to do that? Simply because history has taught us what happens when we do not. This does not mean, however, that Israel should be immune from criticism. One can strongly disagree with policies of the Government of Israel without being called an antisemite.

Nor does it mean that a strong defence of Israel's right to exist and live in security precludes the acceptance of a Palestinian state where all citizens, and in particular young Palestinians, come to know the benefits of health care, educational excellence, economic opportunities, and growing prosperity similar to those available in Israel. This should be the objective of all who believe in justice. And I am certain that, one day relatively soon, we shall see the initiation of a process that will produce precisely this result.

In David Ben-Gurion's epic autobiography, there is a striking quotation on the distinctiveness of Jewish history in the human experience. In the concluding paragraph of his memoirs, he wrote,

> The essence and the significance of Jewish history lies in the preference of quality over quantity. For our security, survival and status in the world, and the preservation of the legacy of our Prophets until the end of time, Israel must strive incessantly for moral, cultural, technological and social improvement and to be a unique people.[14]

James Joyce wrote that 'the past is consumed in the present and the present is alive only because it gives birth to the future.'[15] The Jews of Israel have already emerged as a valorous people who have made the deserts bloom, and the Jews of Canada have found a home whose future is immeasurably brighter and whose values have been incalculably enriched because of their presence and their contribution to Canada and to all mankind.

NOTES

1 Montreal and Kingston: McGill-Queen's University Press, 1998.

2 Ron Rosenbaum, *Explaining Hitler: The Search for the Origins of His Evil* (New York: Random House, 1998), 38.

3 James W. St G. Walker, *'Race,' Rights and the Law in the Supreme Court of Canada: Historical Case Studies* (Toronto: Osgoode Society for Canadian Legal History and the Wilfrid Laurier University Press, 1997), 189.

4 Irving Abella, 'Antisemitism in Canada: New Perspectives on an Old Problem,' in Michael Brown, ed., *Approaches to Antisemitism: Context and Curriculum* (New York and Jerusalem: American Jewish Committee and the International Center for University Teaching of Jewish Civilization, 1994), 46.

5 Ibid., 47.

6 *Diaries of William Lyon MacKenzie King* (MG26-J13), Wednesday, 10 February 1937: 2. Available at http://king.archives.ca.

7 Ibid., Tuesday, 29 June 1937: 10–11.

8 Ibid., Wednesday, 30 June 1937: 4.

9 Ibid., Wednesday, 30 June 1937: 5.

10 Ibid., Thursday, 1 July 1937: 4.

11 Irving Abella and Harold Trooper, *None Is Too Many: Canada and the Jews of Europe 1933–1948*, 3rd ed. (Toronto: Lester Publishing Limited, 1991), xxi.

12 Ibid., 64–5.

13 *Public Papers of the Presidents of the United States: John F. Kennedy, 1963*: 503.

14 David Ben-Gurion, *Israel: A Personal History* (New York: Funk and Wagnalls, 1971), 846.

15 James Joyce, *A Portrait of the Artist as a Young Man* (New York: Viking Press, 1964), 251.

Chapter 2

Law and Antisemitism: The Role for the State in Responding to Hatred

THE HONOURABLE R. ROY McMURTRY

In this essay, the Honourable R. Roy McMurtry, former Attorney General of Ontario and now its chief justice, expresses his commitment to combating antisemitism within the framework of Canada's legal system. The law, he writes, is an expression of the central mores and values of a society. Laws directed against hate propaganda and hate-motivated crime are therefore important not just because they punish and deter hate-mongers, but also because they signal our collective commitment to tolerance and our rejection of racism in all its forms. At the same time, he cautions, the law cannot be a substitute for the individual responsibility we all bear to combat antisemitism and other forms of bigotry. This essay is more than an exhortation, for Chief Justice McMurtry has striven to fulfil the responsibilities he sets before all of us.

* * *

I believe antisemitism to be one of the most vicious diseases ever visited upon the human race. I also believe very strongly that the state has a vital role in combating the dissemination of hatred.

As the Attorney General for Ontario for a decade, I and my ministry made the fight against hatred on the basis of religion or race a priority. For me, the issues of antisemitism and racism are very much linked and represent an almost seamless web of evil.

When I became attorney general in 1975, the pluralistic and demographic nature of Ontario, and of Toronto in particular, was changing rather dramatically. The result was a significant increase in the activities of racist groups like the Western Guard, which was an Ontario version of the Ku Klux Klan. Antisemitism had traditionally been an article of faith for the Western Guard, and the arrival of increased numbers of immigrants of colour motivated the Western Guard to increase their evil activities generally.

As both attorney general and solicitor general, I had no hesitation in urging law enforcement bodies to target these activities, which resulted in arrests, convictions, and the imposition of prison sentences. It is my view that elected officials do have the right and the responsibility to urge police departments to prioritize certain investigations when the public interest will clearly be served. While many hate crimes fall short of physical violence, they are nonetheless equally destructive of our social fabric.

However, it has often been stated that the communication of hatred must be tolerated as a price that society must pay in order to protect fundamental principles related to freedom of speech. For me, the wilful promotion of hatred should never be confused with legitimate freedom of expression.

Many of us will recall the legal debate in Skokie, Illinois, some years ago when the American Civil Liberties Union fought for the right of self-proclaimed Nazi groups to march in that community. I did not then, nor do I now, agree with the position of the ACLU. Rather, I prefer the view of Dag Hammerskjöld, a former secretary general of the United Nations, who once wrote, 'The madman shouted in the market place, but no one stopped to answer him. Thus it was confirmed that his thesis was incontrovertible.'[1] As attorney general, I included the following statement in a number of my speeches:

> It is important to answer the madman. It is important because, left unanswered, his lies and his malice can poison the climate. They can do worse. They can make other men mad. Left unanswered for long enough, they can nourish everything in men and women that is hateful and destructive and murderous.

At the same time, I recognize the regrettable truth that the law alone will probably never be enough to provide protection from malevolent people propelled by hatred for those who are of a different colour or a different religion. The law will never be enough because there is simply no legislature in the world capable of codifying ultimate principles.

In fact, during the debate about whether hate propaganda sections should be added to the Criminal Code, a professor who had long advised the Ontario Human Rights Commission expressed the rather negative opinion that the efficacy of criminal law would always depend upon the strength of a society's moral fabric; and that if Canada embraces racism, occasional prosecutions will be of little avail. Nevertheless, I believed then and still believe that the law, together with the lawmakers, including judges, can express in clear terms the central mores and values of a society. By that I do not mean that they should bow to the various waves of popular opinion that wash back and forth but that our laws should embody, crystallize, and project those fundamental premises upon which a society of free and equal citizens is built and maintained.

In any event, as we know, in 1970 an amendment to the Criminal Code of Canada was passed that made it an offence to advocate or promote genocide against any group of people distinguished by colour, race, religion, or ethnic origin or to communicate statements in a public place inciting hatred against such an identifiable group that is likely to lead to a breach of the peace.[2]

The law is somewhat imperfect, and it was passed by Parliament only after weeks of debate – a debate during which many well-intentioned MPs took it apart, discussed it, and analysed it, clause by clause, in an effort to make certain that it did not conflict with fundamental rights in relation to freedom of speech. And a good many Canadians, with all the goodwill in the world, wondered publicly whether it should ever be passed at all.

The Toronto *Globe and Mail* summed up the reservations held by these people when it said, flatly, in an editorial on 20 February 1970, 'This is *not* an area for legislation.' Many people listened and still listen to that argument.

But the bill passed, and became law, because *more* people listened to an argument put by Maxwell Cohen, former dean of law at McGill University and chairman of the committee that drew up the bill. Dr Cohen, while admitting that the bill was not perfect, urged us to admit that words can do grievous harm to our fellow men, and that we must act upon this knowledge in constructing legislation. And I say, if it is true that no law can stamp out bigotry and hatred and madness, it is equally true that they will flourish the more for lack of any laws against their flourishing.

I also think that it is very well worth repeating the comments of then Minister of Justice John Turner when he introduced the amendments to the Criminal Code:

> What this bill hopes and seeks to articulate is that we condemn the social evil of the deliberate, wilful dissemination of racial hatred in this country and elsewhere. We consider it to be a poison in a civilized society. We consider it to be contrary to the collective moral sense and total integrity of the Canadian people. We consider in the global village in which we are living, which is almost claustrophobic, that the exploitation of hostility in man and the skilful promotion of hatred must be combated. As such, in its ultimate sense the criminal law sanction, and in this context the bill outlawing the dissemination of hate ... is a conscientious attempt on the part of the government, and I hope of Parliament itself, to outlaw as an articulation of the total integrity of the Canadian community the dissemination of hate in this country and throughout the world, proclaiming our commitment to humanity, humanism, and the rule of law.[3]

Notwithstanding the amendments to the Criminal Code, there remained a surprising insensitivity to the issue of hate propaganda in some major Canadian institutions, such as the Bell Telephone Company. People were, in fact, allowed to record antisemitic and white-power messages using the Bell telephone system.

As the Attorney General for Ontario, I was able to persuade the federal government to take action against the recording of these messages, which fell within their legislative jurisdiction. While the government's initial reaction was not encouraging, they ultimately acceded and enacted a provision prohibiting such messages in the *Canadian Human Rights Act*.[4]

At the same time, our courts were somewhat slow to recognize that criminal assaults that were racially or religiously motivated should, for that reason, be treated more seriously in sentencing. In a case that I appealed to the Ontario Court of Appeal in 1977, a trial judge found as a fact that the assault for which two accused were found guilty was completely unprovoked and racially motivated. However, the trial judge specifically stated that he would not take the racial nature of the attack into consideration as an aggravating factor in determining the appropriate sentence. In other words, an assault was simply an assault, regardless of the motivation.

In allowing our Crown appeal, Chief Justice Dubin writing for the court stated,

> It is a fundamental principle of our society that every member must respect the dignity, privacy and person of the other. Crimes of violence increase when respect for the rights of others decreases, and, in that manner, assaults such as occurred in this case attack the very fabric of our society. An assault which is racially motivated renders the offence more heinous. Such assaults, unfortunately, invite imitation and repetition by others and incite retaliation. The danger is even greater in a multicultural, pluralistic urban society. The sentence imposed must be one which expresses the public abhorrence for such conduct and their refusal to countenance it.[5]

Any assault that is motivated by antisemitism should as a result be treated in the same manner. However, it was not until 1996 that the Criminal Code of Canada was amended to reflect the sentencing principle laid down by Chief Justice Dubin.[6]

In 1977, it became evident that certain people were apparently noticing that the Attorney General for Ontario was giving a high priority to the battle against antisemitism in particular and racism in general. I was actually pleased to receive a threatening letter from the Ku Klux Klan which read,

> This letter is in protest against your anti-white policies, which have been in direct opposition to the interests of the white Canadian population of the North American continent.

Specifically, you have sought to destroy the sacred right of freedom of speech for white Canadians. Secondly, you have instructed your subordinates to apply the law unequally to white youths involved in racial incidents. Thirdly, you have betrayed your race and nation by your subservience to international Zionism and the State of Israel. Take heed that your nefarious anti-white activities are being monitored and recorded by our international Klan movement. If you persist in your treacherous activities against the white race, I can assure you that there can only be grave consequences.
In the name of the White Race
David Duke, Grand Wizard
Knights of the Ku Klux Klan[7]

A rather frightening sequel to this letter was the fact that the same David Duke received a significant amount of voter support when he ran to be the governor of Louisiana a few years later.

While I strongly believe in the value of the hate propaganda sections in the Criminal Code, there are often problematic policy issues that must be considered by any attorney general in relation to prosecutions under the sections relating to advocating genocide and the wilful promotion of hatred. Both sections require the consent of the attorney general before any charge can be laid.

The issues that concerned me as an attorney general were basically related to the legal challenges that faced any prosecution, given the highly complex nature of the sections and the platform that would be available and perhaps welcomed by an accused who was a perpetrator of hate propaganda.

An example of this type of policy challenge was whether I should prosecute Ernst Zundel under the wilful promotion of hatred sections. My senior law officers believed that there would be significant legal hurdles, given the very broad defences provided by the legislation. There was, therefore, a real danger of what could be a highly publicized acquittal that could have the effect of encouraging other potential hate-mongers. We also believed that Zundel, in particular, would very much welcome the publicity and the platform that a prosecution would provide.

The Jewish community was clearly and understandably divided on the issue and, in the final analysis, I did not consent to a prosecution. However, a charge was laid privately, under the 'spreading of false news' section, that did not require the consent of the attorney general.[8] This section was ultimately struck down as unconstitutional by the Supreme Court of Canada.[9] In any event, my concerns about giving Zundel enormous publicity became fully realized as a result of the prosecution that took place under that section. I had considered staying the prosecution because of my concerns but decided, rightly or wrongly, that such a step would be misunderstood in the Jewish community.

I also recall another prosecution that we considered, related to a book that was essentially a hate diatribe directed towards Aboriginals in north-western Ontario. There was a reasonable prospect of a conviction, but the Aboriginal leaders who were consulted strongly recommended against a prosecution because of the publicity that would be given to a book that they believed would otherwise quickly fade from the public mind.

We know that anti-hate speech laws are opposed by many advocates of free speech. While I find it impossible to see any redeeming value in the utterances of the hate-monger, it is nevertheless argued that such laws pose an unjustifiable risk to the competing value of freedom of expression.

In *R. v. Keegstra*,[10] a majority of the Supreme Court of Canada held that it was possible to identify with sufficient clarity and precision that which is truly unworthy and reprehensible without posing a significant risk to honest and vigorous debate. All members of the court accepted the argument that the objective of the anti-hate law was sufficiently compelling to justify this limitation of the right of freedom of expression under the Charter of Rights and Freedoms. Such a law was intended to avoid tangible harm in the form of feelings of humiliation and degradation felt by those targeted as well as to enhance a social climate of mutual respect and tolerance. As various means of communication become more available, the challenges relating to combating hatred, of course, increase. For example, hate propaganda promulgated through the Internet poses difficult problems for traditional legal systems. Governments and courts will have to determine how to apply existing anti-hate criteria to novel relationships and forms of communication.

In preparing for these remarks, I encountered an interesting article published by Jeff Brunner in the *Manitoba Law Journal* in 1999 entitled 'Canada's Use of Criminal and Human Rights Legislation to Control Hate Propaganda.'[11] The author writes, 'There are many situations where a Human Rights Tribunal is a more appropriate forum than criminal courts to control hate propaganda. Primarily it is much harder to get a criminal conviction than a Human Rights Tribunal conviction.'[12] The author also observes that 'human rights legislation requires only the civil standard of proof as a balance of probabilities and can apply their own rules of evidence.'[13]

Mr Brunner also notes that human rights legislation has some obvious limitations and flaws but concludes that criminal laws and human rights legislation should coexist.[14] For example, the British Columbia Human Rights Code prohibits publications and statements that are likely to expose a person or group to hatred or contempt because of religion or race. The Ontario Human

Rights Code does not contain a similar prohibition; this might therefore be an amendment that should be considered by the Ontario legislature.

Another article I encountered referred to a survey conducted in 1999 that revealed approximately 273,000 incidents in Canada in which the victim considered the crime to have been motivated by hate. Of these incidents, approximately 43 per cent were directed at individuals on the basis of their race or religion. The authors of the study also concluded that findings of hate motivation have led to heavier sentences in many cases and that the 1996 amendment to the Criminal Code has increased awareness of hate-based crimes in the courts and community.[15]

In conclusion, I would suggest that the law, in the final analysis, is merely an expression of what we stand for and how we want our society to behave. At the same time, the law should never be considered as a substitute for the responsibility of the individual citizen, and that is why this volume is such an important forum for the education of all of our fellow citizens.

NOTES

1 Dag Hammarskjöld, *Markings*, trans. Leif Sjöberg and W.H. Auden (New York: Alfred A. Knopf, 1972), 161.
2 *Criminal Code*, R.S. 1985, c-46, ss.318–19.
3 *House of Commons Debates* (6 April 1970) at 5557.
4 *Canadian Human Rights Act*, R.S. 1985, c.H-6, s.13.
5 *R. v. Ingram*, [1977] O.J. No. 53.
6 *Criminal Code*, R.S. 1985, c-46, s.718.2(a)(i).
7 Received 14 March 1977.
8 *Criminal Code*, R.S. 1985, c-46, s.181.
9 *R. v. Zundel*, [1992] 2 S.C.R. 731.
10 *R. v. Keegstra*, [1996] 1 S.C.R. 458.
11 J. Brunner, 'Canada's Use of Criminal and Human Rights Legislation to Control Hate Propaganda,' *Manitoba Law Journal* 26 (1999): 299.
12 Ibid., 310.
13 Ibid.
14 Ibid., 315.
15 Canadian Centre for Justice Statistics, *Criminal Victimization in Canada 1999*. Available online from Statistics Canada at http://www.communityaccounts.ca/ communityaccounts/onlinedata/relatedsites/victimization.pdf

PART II

Scholars on Antisemitism, New and Old

Chapter 3

The Changing Dimensions of Contemporary Canadian Antisemitism

MORTON WEINFELD

How should one evaluate antisemitism in Canada today? By some measures, Jews have never done better in this country. Looked at from the vantage points of political, economic, and cultural success, Jews are impressively well off. Opinion polls are less conclusive, but on the whole such surveys suggest steady improvements – and certainly indicate that many other groups fare less well than Jews. Overall, Professor Weinfeld reports, if one uses traditional indicators one would believe that Canadian antisemitism has been on the decline since the 1950s. Paradoxically, however, Canadian Jews feel insecure. Part of the reason for this has to do with a disturbing rise in antisemitic incidents, however difficult these are to assess and measure scientifically. Perceptions do matter, however. Particularly with respect to Israel, Canadian Jewry – or a good part of it, at least – feels threatened and besieged. In this chapter, Professor Morton Weinfeld examines the reasons for this seeming paradox, reports on how social scientists have come to grips with it, and suggests how the rest of us might think about it.

* * *

Definitions

Antisemitism in Canada is changing. As many of the traditional forms have declined – though not disappeared – newer forms have emerged. The newer manifestations relate to issues of 'reasonable accommodation,' and, more seriously, to the use in many cases of animus towards Israel and Zionism as surrogates for traditional anti-Jewish expression.

I define antisemitism as views or actions (including inactions) that are, or that most Jews perceive as, harmful. This definition is agnostic regarding motivations, focusing more on consequences than intentions. By including the perceptions of victims, it introduces a subjectivity that some might find problematic. After all, Jews can be paranoid, or simply mistaken, about perceived antisemitism. Moreover, some Jews might be opportunistic and label as antisemitic legitimate criticism of Israeli policy. Why not rely on 'the usual suspects,' such as objective behavioural measures and overtly hostile attitudes (see below) and leave subjective considerations aside?

The reason is that social scientific studies of racism now recognize that the voice of the victim deserves to be heard. This is particularly true since most objective indicators of racism or antisemitism might no longer accurately portray what is going on or what may happen in the future. Racism is politically incorrect. Moreover, much of it is subtle and systemic. So survey respondents and Canadians generally might not openly express it.

As a result, analysts of contemporary racism, and discrimination generally, add to their roster of measures the notions of harassment directed at racial minorities, women, and gays. The sociological and legal literature on such harassment recognizes that the harms at issue may flow unintentionally from actions of perpetrators. Such actions may also create a 'chilly climate' or adverse work environment that penalizes minorities of all sorts.[1]

Most liberals and progressives would not dismiss out of hand the subjective perceptions of victims of racism, sexism, or homophobia. Indeed, the law now stipulates that such claims of harassment – whether in the academy or in the workplace – must be investigated to see if they are valid. Alleged victims are not initially dismissed as paranoid or ideologically partisan. They are given the benefit of the doubt. Why not extend the same logic to Jews who perceive antisemitism?

In addition, the range of indicators of antisemitism has expanded to include public policy positions in various domains. This parallels developments in the study of racism generally. In the United States, opposition to affirmative action, and in Canada, opposition to expansive immigration levels are seen – at times rightly and at times wrongly – as expressions of racism. The same logic can apply to opposition to Israeli policies, which – depending on the case at hand – may or may not be antisemitic in motivation or consequence.

Legal or *de jure* antisemitism refers to two types. The first is explicit law that is directly aimed at causing harm to Jews. The Nuremberg laws in Nazi Germany, the apartheid laws in South Africa, or the Chinese head tax in Canada would be examples aimed at Jews or other minorities. Such laws no longer exist in Canada. In fact, human rights acts and the Charter of Rights and Freedoms itself ally the state explicitly with minorities and against discrimination – though critical legal theorists would argue that the legal inequalities continue in more subtle forms.

The second type refers to legal interpretation, often via the courts. Much of this revolves, as indicated, around 'reasonable accommodation,' rooted in potential clashes of conflicting rights or differing cultural traditions. Such accommodations have evolved. Up until the early 1960s at McGill, regular classes were routinely held on Saturdays. This obviously penalized Orthodox Jewish students. Now all McGill faculty get an email every year reminding them to be culturally sensitive to all kinds of religions – including Wicca – and to accommodate their religious calendars for tests and assignments.

Courts must decide how far the majority community must go to accommodate the religious and cultural concerns of all minorities, including Jews. In one example, Le Sanctuaire, a posh, high-rise condo in Montreal, sought a permanent injunction from the Quebec Superior Court against Orthodox residents who built a *sukkah* – a makeshift wood hut with branches for a roof – on their balconies during the holiday of Sukkot. The issue of religious freedom was at stake, at least for the Jewish condo owners. Other residents objected to the defacement of the property. To adjudicate the case, the court heard conflicting expert testimony from two rabbis, and eventually the court decided for Le Sanctuaire. The court agreed with their rabbi that residents could use the *sukkah* at local synagogues. So no *sukkah*s at Le Sanctuaire – though, as of early 2004, the case was under appeal and was to be heard by the Supreme Court.[2]

Such cases, far removed from overt antisemitism, are likely to proliferate, and their judicial outcomes will help determine the parameters of defensible Canadian Jewish interests. A more serious example would be a court challenge to male circumcision on grounds of cruelty to children.[3] Should a court in Canada decide to criminalize Jewish ritual circumcision, many Jews would construe this as antisemitic in consequence if not intent, and many would choose protest, civil disobedience, and breaking the law as a response.

Measures and Indicators of Antisemitism

Most forms of antisemitism are clearly illegal and socially unacceptable and do not rest on judicial interpretation. *Antisemitic incidents* can include speech acts, some of which in Canada can qualify as hate speech, as well as acts of violence or outright discrimination. B'nai Brith provides annual counts of acts, and over the past years they have risen, though not in linear fashion. In the 1980s when these data were first collected, the incidents numbered in the eighties or nineties. The numbers have risen steadily. For the year 2002, the number reached 459, which included a troubling 60 per cent jump over the figures for 2001. The long-term rise has been helped by better reporting; the dramatic recent one-year gain was likely caused, in the view of B'nai Brith officials, by tensions in the Middle East related to the Second Intifada.[4]

Most of these incidents are private. They range from acts of vandalism against Jewish property, to assaults, to threats, to uttering antisemitic slurs. Some acts, like discrimination against a Jewish job applicant, might never be discovered and would not be included in these counts.

A few acts are public, or become public, and resound through the Canadian Jewish community. Examples include the trials of Holocaust deniers Jim Keegstra, an Alberta schoolteacher, or Ernst Zundel, a Toronto-based publisher, in the 1980s. More recently we have events such as the riot at Concordia University in September of 2002 that led to the cancellation of a speech by Israeli former prime minister Binyamin Netanyahu; viciously anti-Jewish comments that seemingly justified the Holocaust by Saskatchewan Aboriginal leader David Ahenakew in December of 2002; or the attempted cancellation of a speech by the pro-Israeli Middle Eastern expert Daniel Pipes at York University in January of 2003.

All of these high-profile incidents are filtered through the Canadian media. On cases of explicit antisemitism, as in the case of David Ahenakew, the media tend to reflect the hurt and outrage felt by Jews and indeed most Canadians. On cases dealing with the Middle East, where actions can take the gloss of protest against Israeli policy, the possibility of anti-Israel bias on the part of some Canadian media might complicate understanding and the impact of such events. Norman Spector, former Canadian ambassador to Israel, took the unprecedented step of publicly accusing the Canadian Broadcasting Corporation of a systematic anti-Israel bias in its Middle East coverage. This bias, Spector argued, in turn helped to spread currents of antisemitism.[5]

Attitudes and social behaviours are other indicators measuring antisemitism. Surveys measuring belief in antisemitic stereotypes and the preferred social distance from Jews are used often. Since the Second World War there has been a general decline in the Canadian public in anti-Jewish attitudes. Still, one survey in 1984 estimated that one-seventh of Canadians held negative attitudes about Jews. This survey found antisemitism to be more pronounced in Newfoundland, New Brunswick, and Quebec – and less so in Alberta, among Catholics and French-speakers, and among those with lower levels of education.[6] Another survey found that levels of antisemitic prejudice decreased with higher levels of social contact with Jews.[7]

In the 1980s Canadian surveys found 20 to 30 per cent agreeing to antisemitic stereotypes, such as 'most Jews are pushy.'[8] And in 1991 64 per cent of Canadians said they were 'very comfortable' around Jews, more than around Sikhs or blacks, but less than around other Europeans or even Chinese at 69 per cent.[9] A 1995 Canadian survey found 14 per cent of Canadians believing Jews had 'too much power,' while Asians came in at 16 per cent, and both blacks and whites at 9 per cent.[10] And B'nai Brith surveys have found that single-digit proportions of Canadians indicate they would not vote for a Jew.[11]

It is hard to know what to make of such surveys. On the one hand they may all understate the level of antisemitism, since most Canadians know that prejudice and discrimination are politically incorrect in the new multicultural Canada. They may hide their resentments, or express them only on matters related to Israel. Are these numbers alarming, or cause for celebration? If one antisemite in Canada is too many, then even the observed percentages are troubling.

But we also have to ask whether these attitudes are translated into discriminatory behaviours. Or are they matters of taste, with little consequence? If someone believes, say, that Jews stick together, or look after their own, is that antisemitism or a sociological observation? A 1990 survey of Canadian Jews found that nearly 80 per cent indicated they had mainly Jewish friends.[12] Moreover, surveys of Jews and other minorities might well yield similar levels of prejudice against majority Canadians.

A related indicator is residential concentration. Usually such concentrations are associated with poverty, and with discrimination on the part of realtors, renters, or vendors. Jews are not poor, but they are by far the most residentially concentrated of any minority group in Canada's cities.[13] But this concentration is today a result of choice rather than coercion. Jews simply prefer to live near other Jews.

One way to understand what survey results really mean is through establishing baselines and trends. This would require annual surveys of antisemitic attitudes, using the same questions and same methodology. No data remotely like this exist in Canada.

Other measures show clear improvements. In annual Canadian national surveys conducted from 1975 to 1995, sociologist Reginald Bibby found a steady increase in the openness to Jewish and non-Jewish marriages, from 80 per cent to 90 per cent. These attitudes have been accompanied by a steady increase in the actual rate of mixed marriage for Jews, from over 10 per cent in the early 1960s to over 30 per cent in the late 1990s.[14] Gentiles would rather marry Jews than harm them.

Victimization surveys ask minorities about their actual experiences and perceptions. Wording and definitions are key in deciding what being victimized by antisemitism can mean. Seeing bathroom graffiti is one thing, being denied a job or being assaulted on the street quite another. A 1996 survey of Montreal Jews touched on perceptions of antisemitism. About 15 per cent said there was a 'great deal' of antisemitism in Quebec. Only 15 per cent had experienced antisemitism in the past two years, and 63 per cent had no direct experience of it at all in Quebec.[15] Here, as in other surveys, the proportions of those personally experiencing antisemitism are lower than of those perceiving that it exists.

Attitude surveys, whether of all Canadians or of Jews, have a subjective element to them. Traditional and more objective indicators of antisemitism measure the *statistical representation* of Jews in the higher economic, cultural, and political sectors of Canadian society. Such contemporary data show that Jews certainly enjoy equal opportunity in Canada. The issue is important given recent Canadian history, when certain economic sectors – banking and insurance – were closed to Jews, elite private clubs excluded them, universities operated quotas against Jewish students and had few Jewish senior professors and administrators, and the political system of the 1930s and 1940s was permeated with antisemitism and antisemites.[16]

Jewish educational, occupational, and income levels today are well above the Canadian average. Indeed, Jews even earn more than might be expected based on their educational and occupational credentials alone. In 1991, over 50 per cent of Jews aged 25 to 34 had at least a bachelor's degree, compared to the Canadian average of 16 per cent. About 22 per cent of Jews lived in households with an income of over $100,000, triple the rate for all Canadians. Only part of these gaps could be explained by Jewish concentrations in Canada's major cities, where incomes are higher. Moreover, Jews are now found well represented among the CEOs of Canada's major corporations – an estimated 8 per cent in the mid-1990s – and among any lists of the wealthiest Canadians.[17]

Jews are also well represented among the political and cultural elites of Canada. (While doing well, they are not as fully integrated as American Jews. This is the result in part of the fact that 30 per cent of Canadian Jews through the 1990s were foreign born, compared to only 10 per cent in the United States. American Jews enjoy a much greater critical mass, between 5 and 5.5 million compared to about 350,000 in Canada, and comprise 1.8 per cent of the American population compared to about 1.2 per cent in Canada. There are about ten Jewish U.S. senators out of 100 compared to only five Jewish MPs out of 295. There are two Jews on the current – 2003 – U.S. Supreme Court, and only one, appointed in 2003, in Canada.) There has been one Jewish provincial premier – Dave Barrett of British Columbia – but three Jewish mayors of Toronto – Nathan Phillips, Phil Givens, and Mel Lastman. Jews have also been represented in the federal cabinet. Perhaps equally important, Jews – Mel Cappe, Eddy Goldenberg, Stanley Hartt, Chaviva Hosek, Hugh Segal, Norman Spector, David Zussman – have been prominent as senior public servants and advisers to Canadian prime ministers in recent years. Canadian culture, notably in its Anglophone variant, is no longer closed to Jewish voices, whether as artists or as cultural entrepreneurs.[18] The list is long and diverse.

To conclude, almost all the traditional indicators – with the exception of reported incidents – suggest that Canadian antisemitism has been declining since the 1950s and is relatively low by comparative standards. Nevertheless, there is a palpable concern, felt right across many segments of the Canadian Jewish community, that antisemitism is a real and growing danger. How to explain this paradox, often cited as the popular lament, If everything is so good, why is everything so bad? Perhaps it flows from the subliminal awareness among Jews that even with high degrees of economic, cultural, and social integration, Jewish security is not guaranteed. After all, the example of Weimar Germany still resonates.

To begin the interpretation of antisemitism in Canadian life, we must remind ourselves that, to paraphrase the sociologist Ben Halpern, 'North America Is Different.'[19] Canada, like the United States, does not have a legacy of pogroms, the Holocaust, and the multilayered 'Jewish Question.'

An anecdote can illustrate this difference. Some months after September 2001 I attended a conference on immigration in Western Europe. At a cocktail reception several of the delegates were chatting informally, and I happened to mention my research on Canadian Jewish topics and my own personal involvement in Canadian Jewish life. After the circle broke up, one of the participants approached me privately. This was a senior professor and administrator at a Western European university, in his mid- to late fifties. The professor, speaking in a quiet voice, expressed his shock at the ease with which I had been talking about these Jewish themes. In a lowered voice, he admitted, 'I too am a Jew, but would never have talked as freely.' The professor went on to say that most of his university colleagues did not know he was Jewish. And even among the few who did, he would very rarely talk about Jewish or Israeli matters. His wife was also Jewish and, like him, born into a European Jewish family that survived the Holocaust. They both decided to raise their child with no connection to Jewishness at all. He sighed. 'Maybe that was a mistake ... but it is too late.'

This kind of frightened insecurity about one's Jewish identity may be atypical, but it is still far more likely to exist in Europe than in multicultural Canada.

Yet many Canadian Jews fear that a 'chilly climate' is spreading regarding the defence of Jewish or Israeli interests. And so they ponder whether, in the future, Canadian Jewish life may move from self-confidence to this European ambivalence. Something new seems afoot. Harvard president Larry Summers warns publicly in September 2002 about the revival of antisemitism on campus. American journalist and civil libertarian Nat Hentoff is quoted in a May 2002 article in *New York* that he would not be surprised one morning to hear loudspeakers 'ordering all Jews to gather in Times Square.' In Canada, *Globe and Mail* science columnist Stephen Strauss writes an anguished April 2002 column on the spectre of antisemitism. And in 2003 former prime minister Brian Mulroney delivers a long address – unprecedented for a former prime minister – focused uniquely on the past and present dangers of antisemitism in Canada.

Are these insecurities paranoia, a kind of gathering hysteria? Or are they simply prudence? Predicting the Jewish future is extremely difficult. We are in the realm of intuition rather than extrapolation from current data. The conventional sociological indicators cited earlier will likely not register the fact and the cause of these new apprehensions. Perhaps they are flying beneath the radar of conventional social science.

In any case, social scientists have a dismal record at predicting any of the major social or political changes affecting Jewish life in the twentieth century.

In 1900 no scholar predicted that today the United States and Israel would be the two centres of Jewish learning and population, and that the major centres in Europe would be gone. None anticipated that Germany would unleash the horror of Nazism and antisemitism (why not France or Russia?). No scholar in 1950 could have predicted that in North America today Orthodoxy and even ultra-Orthodoxy would be vital and growing as a movement, that mixed marriage would be so common, that North American campuses today would see an explosion in Jewish studies courses and programs and Jews as leaders of universities like Harvard or McGill.

Who would have predicted in the 1960s that the most steadfast contemporary defenders of Israel, no longer the land of the kibbutz and the Histadrut and Labour party dominance, would be on the Christian and political right – Reform party/Canadian Alliance/Conservative party – and detractors would be found on the left, from the NDP to academics, as well as among some visible minority groups? Similarly, no one would have foreseen in the early 1960s that the condemnation of Israel could consume so much of the time and energy of the United Nations. No analyst predicted campus boycotts and divestment campaigns against Israeli speakers or investments – but not against the many other more blatant and egregious human rights violators around the planet. This is the newest version of the historic strain of populist and progressive antisemitism, an antisemitism of the left, in which Jews are condemned as capitalist exploiters of the weak and the poor.

In Canada today, left-liberal hard-line critics of Israeli policies find themselves in bed with knee-jerk and reflexive demonizers of Israel, who include some of the most unsavoury, undemocratic, violent, dictatorial, misogynist, homophobic, and generally illiberal regimes and groups anywhere. While this does not invalidate such criticism, it might invite further reflection. This unforeseen political realignment has been agonizing for liberal Jews in general and Zionists in particular, who find themselves increasingly isolated on the political spectrum.

What Is New about Contemporary Canadian Antisemitism?

It is important to distinguish between *Canadian antisemitism* and *antisemitism in Canada*. The former refers to the traditional motifs of Canadian antisemitism. Social Credit and western populism; the unique sources of French antisemitism, rooted in Catholicism and French Quebec nationalism; and the old-line genteel Anglo resentment of and discomfort with Jews that used to manifest itself in social, cultural, and economic exclusion – these are all examples of traditional themes within Canadian antisemitism.

Antisemitism in Canada refers to worldwide trends in antisemitism that have an impact on Canada as well as other societies. It reflects the globalization of antisemitism. This globalization refers to multiple phenomena: the movement of peoples – as migrants, refugees, and visitors – around the world and into Canada as well; the increased salience of the Middle East conflict in Canada as articulated through diaspora Jewish/Israeli and Arab/Muslim communities, increasingly mobilized on foreign policy matters; the role of the Internet and communications generally in multiplying the impact of antisemitic acts (such as the beheading of journalist Daniel Pearl), in linking anti-Jewish and anti-Israeli forces, and in providing competing sources of information and world views. Both Jews and their enemies are now virtual communities.

The proliferation of armed guards in recent years at Jewish schools and synagogues in Canada on major holidays (in Europe, they are present throughout the year) is a consequence of the new globalized antisemitism. Threats of violent attacks directed at Jewish institutions – such as those in Buenos Aires in the 1990s – are more likely to reflect Middle East grievances than to flow from home-grown Canadian antisemitic groups.

The central aspect of this new globalized antisemitism is the link – often debated – among antisemitism, anti-Zionism, and opposition to Israeli policies. There are no definitive polls. But one assumes that for those Canadian Jews who are very committed to Israel's security and survival, these three elements are in some ways related. Within much antisemitic discourse, Israel has replaced Jews as the enemy.

Anti-Zionism and Antisemitism

It is important to explore this asserted nexus in some detail. By anti-Zionism, I refer to the principled opposition to the legitimate existence of the Jewish state of Israel, and support for efforts to dismantle the state or undermine its existence.

Before the creation of Israel, there was very little clear and consistent linkage between anti-Zionism and antisemitism. Most Reform Jews in Western Europe and North America, and many religious Jews throughout the Jewish world, were opposed to Zionism, albeit for different reasons. Reform Jews did not like its nationalism, while some Orthodox and ultra-Orthodox rejected its secular and progressive orientation.

Some philo-Semites also had reservations. American social scientist Thorstein Veblen described in 1919 his fear that that the success of Zionism would deprive Europe and Christendom of a supply of 'renegade Jews' who would continue to contribute to the intellectual and scientific creativity of the West. He feared the normalization of the Jewish people that Zionism would bring.[20]

Things changed after the creation of the state in 1948. In the present, one can argue that anti-Zionism and antisemitism are indelibly linked. This is because support for the anti-Zionist position leads to the defence of positions that are devastating to the well-being of Israeli Jews.

What of academics or pundits who advocate the creation of a single democratic/secular and thus non-Zionist and non-Jewish state? They are not arguing only against the Israeli occupation of the Territories. When they say 'Free Palestine,' or 'End the Occupation,' the terrorist groups, their state sponsors, and their theorizing intellectual soulmates, mean Tel Aviv. In theory, this seems like the expression of a neutral ideological position, and many assert that Israeli Jews would be better off. Theory is one thing, reality another.

In fact, such intellectual anti-Zionism provides cover and respectability to all those terrorist groups and states that seek actively to attack and eventually destroy Israel. This anti-Zionist position does not exist in a real-world vacuum. There are terrorist groups all too eager to use violence to achieve that objective, even if anti-Zionist intellectuals refrain.

The anti-Zionist position is antisemitic because it denies to the Jewish people the right to national liberation and self-determination, rights accorded to most other peoples. It goes so far as to deny to Jews their peoplehood. In the words of Dr Martin Luther King, Jr,

You declare, my friend, that you do not hate Jews, you are merely 'anti-Zionist' ... When people criticize Zionism, they mean Jews ...

Zionism is nothing less than the dream and ideal of the Jewish people returning to live in their own land. How easy it should be for anyone who holds dear this inalienable right of all mankind to understand and support the right of the Jewish People to live in their ancient land of Israel ...

And what is anti-Zionist? It is the denial to the Jewish people of a fundamental right that we justly claim [for the people of Africa] and freely accord all other nations of the globe. It is discrimination against Jews, my friend, because they are Jews. In short, it is antisemitism.[21]

In earlier decades, opponents of Israel were very careful to couch their discourse as anti-Zionist or anti-Israel. Now, as any visitor to militant Islamist websites or reader of bin Laden missives can attest, that distinction has stopped. Talk is of 'the Jews.'

The anti-Zionist and antisemitic link makes for strange bedfellows. Holocaust denier Ernst Zundel has long peddled the notion of a Jewish conspiracy to wage a war against Islam. Holocaust denier and British Columbia journalist Doug Collins linked the fabrication of the myth of the Holocaust (he used the term 'Swindler's List') to efforts by Zionists and Jews, active in Hollywood, to garner sympathy for Israel.[22] And former Alberta schoolteacher Jim Keegstra instructed his Canadian high school students about the links of the ongoing Jewish conspiracy to Israel. As one of his students wrote, reflecting the notes taken in class, 'The Jews believe that by the year 2000 they will control the world ... They want to set up their new world order with the headquarters in Israel.'[23]

In brief, I argue that the continued, aggressive advocacy of the anti-Zionist position – through debate, boycotts, and terror – aids and abets the potential genocide of the Jewish Israeli population.

Israeli Jews can react to the anti-Zionist proposition in two ways. They can come to accept it after debate, democratically, and vote to reconstruct their Jewish state of Israel, and live as an eventual minority in a Palestinian/Islamic state run by Arafat or Islamist groups like Hamas or both. Obviously that is unlikely, at least in the foreseeable future. Israeli Jews, like most readers of this chapter, would likely not prefer to live in such a state. They know that minorities of all sorts fare poorly in non-liberal states with Arab and/or Islamic majorities. This would be most true for Jews, who have been demonized in those societies for decades.

Alternatively, Israeli Jews can resist that idea, in which case they will encounter active and violent opposition in various forms. Israel could experience, if not military defeat, then unacceptable levels of violence, whether in conventional terror attacks, suicide bombings, or perhaps new chemical, biological, or dirty nuclear forms. The combined intellectual and terrorist onslaught can also lead to a demoralization of the Israeli Jewish population and economic decline, in which case many might leave. This is not far-fetched. Exile or dispersion is not unknown in Jewish history, whether in 70 CE or 1492. And, of course, those who do not leave may die defending their Israeli homeland. In either event, with the exception of some ultra-Orthodox and ultra-leftists, Israel/Palestine would become *Judenrein.*

Criticism of Israeli Policy

There is no clear link between antisemitism and criticism of Israeli policy. There is no automatic tie, since the Israeli press, universities, living rooms, and Knesset are full of such criticism. Jews who see themselves as lovers of Zion are themselves sharply divided, from left to right. The charge of antisemitism should never be used as a knee-jerk response to stifle vigorous criticism and debate about Israeli policies.

But there are occasions when harsh, one-sided criticism of Israeli policies is indeed antisemitic in its consequences, and possibly in motive. Many criticisms of Israeli policies are not made for any constructive purpose – how to move both sides to a fair and realistic compromise solution, that is, a two-state solution – but to delegitimate Israel itself. In fact these criticisms often have a fervour that borders on Zionophobia or Israelophobia.[24]

Consider the time, energy, and number of resolutions devoted by the United Nations to condemning Israeli policy.[25] The Durban antiracism conference seemed to many Canadian Jews a one-sided festival of Israel-bashing. Such efforts seem out of all proportion, given the number of other major conflicts and human rights violations on which the United Nations is routinely and deafeningly silent. This apparent obsession with Israel can be seen as seeking to delegitimate the very existence of Israel. Consider the divestment campaigns or the academic boycotts of Israel and Israeli academics. Again, why focused on Israel? The new antisemitic discourse leads through Israel and the Middle East, and reflects a double standard.

And as Israel is attacked, Jews are attacked for being supporters of Israel. This critique of Zionism, Israel, and its Jewish supporters may also gain strength – particularly in Europe – because it can reduce the Holocaust guilt of both perpetrators and bystanders. Europeans can claim, 'We may have been evil in the past, but look at these Israelis and Jews, they are (comparably?) evil now.'

Criticism of Israel – even legitimate criticism – also runs into the anti-Zionist and thus antisemitic shadow. The question is one of volume. As the drumbeat of criticism against Israel grows louder, as Israel is painted as a pariah among nations, like apartheid South Africa, the option of using coercion to transform the state begins to look more acceptable.

Given the legacy of the Holocaust, some Jews are inevitably thin-skinned, hypersensitive, and will at times conflate legitimate criticism of Israeli policies – the continuing proliferation of the settlements, the brutalities of the occupation – with antisemitism. Those Jews who see Israel as relatively weak may be more likely to see criticism as antisemitic.

So how can Canadians criticize Israeli policies without being called antisemitic?

It should be stressed that people – Jews and non-Jews alike – have the right to criticize Israeli policy without fear of moral censorship. But equally, others have the right to question the motivations and consequences of that criticism. Jews have ample reasons for being sensitive, not just because of the Holocaust. More recently, chilling episodes of Jew hatred – the beheading of American journalist Daniel Pearl, the glee of the mob at the blood-drenched hands of one of the murderers of two Israelis inside a Ramallah police station, the widespread conspiratorial belief throughout the Arab/Muslim world that Jews/Israel were behind the 11 September 2001 terror attack – resonate among Jews.

It is easy for academics and commentators who criticize Israel to establish their bona fides – though there is no reason why they have to do this. Critics of Israeli policy need not pass any litmus test. But for those who choose to do so, options are clear. If their criticism is situated within a framework designed to lead to a fair, just, and reasonable two-state solution, and if the criticism avoids placing all blame for the current Middle East stalemate on the Israeli side – personal attacks on the critics would be clearly unjustified.

The Changing Environment for Canadian Jews

Changing Canadian demographics have changed the social environment within this new globalized context of antisemitism. The Canadian Jewish population is growing slowly, while Arab and Muslim communities are growing rapidly, mainly through recent immigration. This is part of the general increase in the visible minority population since the 1960s. These demographic changes are noticeable on Canadian campuses and in major cities, especially Montreal and Toronto.

Jews through their organizations have long played a role in the historic struggle for equal rights for all minorities in Canada.[26] But within the antiracist coalition in Canada it may be harder to make common cause between Jews and visible minorities. First, the type of racism each suffers is very different. Jews are white, more established, and economically successful, and are attacked for their perceived power and suspect loyalties. Visible minorities encounter overt and systemic racism, often intertwined with poverty and immigrant status.

Second, different positions on the Middle East or on the war against terror-ism may polarize relations among potential allies. This is particularly likely given the different historical baggage of the European and the newer non-European immigrants. For the former, Jewish or not, the Holocaust, the struggles against fascism and even communism, and the creation of Israel are part of a common historical experience. This is not the case for immigrants from Asia, the Middle East, Africa, and the Caribbean, who have their own genocidal tragedies as part of their heritage and who see Israel and Jews as victors rather than victims. In short, the antiracist Canadian coalition may experience the fracture that broke the black-Jewish liberal alliance in the United States. Tensions that emerged over the showing of the allegedly racist play *Showboat* in Toronto in the 1990s prefigure such a rupture.[27]

The global political environment has also worsened for Canadian Jews. Attacks on Israeli policies have led to greater isolation for the Jewish community, and for liberal Jews in particular. The latter feel not only discomfort with the aggressive policies of the Sharon government but abandonment by former allies on the left. This trend has intensified since 1967. In the prevailing progressive discourse on geopolitics, Israel is seen as Western/colonial, white, and tied to the United States – three serious strikes.

The Israeli tie to the United States is a key element in the new globalized antisemitism. Attacks on American policy on Iraq or throughout the developing world can shade into attacks on Israel, and then on Israel's supporters – Jews. Antiglobalization and peace rallies on Iraq feature placards jointly attacking both George W. Bush and Ariel Sharon. After 11 September 2001 and the Second Intifada, it might be argued that the United States and Israel are joined in a common struggle against terror that has enhanced the real and perceived links between the two countries.

In this sense Canadian Jews may feel more isolated than their American counterparts. The United States has for years been recognized as Israel's staunchest ally and supporter. The United States is more likely to vote with Israel – often alone – on contentious UN resolutions, whereas for Canada abstentions have been the more 'even-handed' response. The reflexive anti-Americanism found among many in Canada's political and cultural elite works to further isolate Canadian Jews on the conflict with Iraq and the Israeli-Palestinian dispute. The growth of anti-Americanism in Canada will work to the detriment of Canadian Jews who support Israel.

Indeed, globalization concerns have given new life to traditional antisemitic staples such as the charge of dual loyalty and a Jewish-Zionist conspiracy. The allegation that the Bush government's hostility to Iraq is driven by a cabal involving the Israeli government and hawkish American Jews has moved from antisemitic websites to respected newspaper columns and television opinion shows. *Globe and Mail* columnist Jeffrey Simpson glibly refers to 'Likudniks' in the Bush administration.[28]

Canadian antisemitism today is not the antisemitism of the past. Traditional forms of religious, economic, cultural, and social discrimination are declining, though the recent spike in reported incidents is alarming. Policies and court decisions dealing with reasonable accommodation will increase. But the single decisive challenge for Canadian Jews in the future will be on the posture Canada adopts on matters relating to Israeli security and Middle East peace, and possible roles of Canadian Jews in shaping, supporting, or challenging those policies.

Antisemitism today acts and flows through Israel, and reflects global forces and ideologies. Many Canadian Jews, antennae habitually set on high, sense a chillier climate ahead, despite the objective gains in so many other areas.[29]

NOTES

1 See Frances Henry, Carol Tator, Winston Mattis, Tim Rees, *The Colour of Democracy: Racism in Canadian Society*, 2nd ed. (Toronto: Harcourt Brace, 2000).

2 Morton Weinfeld, *Like Everone Else ... But Different: The Paradoxical Success of Canadian Jews* (Toronto: McClelland and Stewart, 2001), 273–4.

3 Ibid., 274.

4 Canadian Press, 'Anti-Semitic Incidents Up 60% : B'nai Brith,' *The Gazette*, 7 March 2003: A10.

5 Mr Spector summarized his complaints in an open letter to Tony Burman of the CBC in the *National Post*, 8 January 2003. Subsequently, an attempt to organize a debate between Mr Spector and Mr Burman to be broadcast on CBC TV itself proved unsuccessful.

6 Robert Brym and Rhonda Lenton, 'The Distribution of Antisemitism in Canada in 1984,' in Robert Brym, William Shaffir, Marton Weinfeld, et al., eds, *The Jews in Canada* (Toronto: Oxford University Press, 1993), 112–20.

7 Gabriel Weimann and Conrad Winn, *Hate on Trial* (Oakville, ON: Mosaic Press, 1986), 115, 152.

8 Jeffrey Reitz and Raymond Breton, *The Illusion of Difference* (Toronto: C.D. Howe Institute, 1994), 72.

9 J.W. Berry and R. Kalin, 'Multicultural and Ethnic Attitudes in Canada: An Overview of the 1991 National Survey,' *Canadian Journal of Behavioral Science* 27 (1995): 301–20.

10 Reginald Bibby, *The Bibby Report: Social Trends, Canadian Style* (Toronto Stoddart, 1995), 55.

11   Taylor Buckner, 'Attitudes Toward Minorities: Seven Year Results and Analysis' (Montreal: League for Human Rights of B'nai Brith, 1991).
12   Jay Brodbar, et al., 'An Overview of the Canadian Jewish Community,' in Brym, Shaffir, Weinfeld, et al., eds, *The Jews in Canada*, 54.
13   Weinfeld, *Like Everyone Else ... But Different*, 165–8.
14   Ibid., 374–5.
15   Charles Shahar, *A Survey of Jewish life in Montreal* (Montreal: Federation of Jewish Community Services, Dec. 1996), 34–5.
16   For a discussion of antisemitism through Canadian history see Alan Davies, ed., *Antisemitism in Canada: History and Interpretation* (Waterloo, ON: Wilfrid Laurier University Press, 1992).
17   Weinfeld, *Like Everyone Else ... But Different*, 102–7.
18   Ibid., ch. 7.
19   Ben Halpern's 'America Is Different' is found in M. Sklare, ed., *The Jew in American Society* (New York: Behrman House, 1974), 67–92.
20   Thorstein Veblen, 'The Intellectual Pre-eminence of Jews in Modern Europe,' *Political Science Quarterly*, 34 (1919): 3–42.
21   Martin Luther King Jr, 'Letter to an Anti-Zionist Friend' *Saturday Review*, xlvii (August 1967): 76.
22   For a review of the Collins case, see my *Like Everyone Else ... But Different*, 331–7.
23   Steve Mertl and John Ward, *Keegstra* (Saskatoon: Western Producer Prairie Books, 1985), 12.
24   Thanks to Professor Gil Troy of the McGill History Department for suggesting the use of these two terms. A recent study of antisemitism in Britain echoes many of the views developed in this section. See Barry Kosmin and Paul Iganski, eds, *A New Antisemitism? Debating Judeophobia in 21st Century Britain* (London: Institute for Jewish Policy Research, 2003).
25   Anne Bayefsky, 'Israel's Second Class Status at the UN,' *National Post*, 18 February 2003; and 'Gentleman's Agreement at the UN,' *Globe and Mail*, 23 December 2002.
26   James W. St G. Walker, '*Race*,' *Rights, and the Law in the Supreme Court of Canada: Historical Case Studies* (Toronto: Osgoode Society for Canadian Legal History and Wilfrid Laurier University Press, 1997).
27   See Howard Adelman, 'Blacks and Jews: Race, Antisemitism and *Showboat*,' in Howard Adelman and John Simpson, eds, *Multiculturalism, Jews, and Identities in Canada* (Jerusalem: Magnes Press, 1996), 128–78.
28   Ami Eden, 'Israel's Role: The Elephant They're Talking About,' *The Forward*, 23 February 2003: 1, 17; Jeffrey Simpson, 'The American Dream Paradox,' *Globe and Mail*, 4 March 2003.

29 In remarks delivered in Montreal in June 2003 to 900 attendees at a Jewish
   National Fund dinner, industrialist Peter Munk, a Jew who managed to escape
   Central Europe before the Holocaust, articulated these fears. He referred repeat-
   edly to Jews as a 'fringe' group that was both 'dispensable' and 'disposable.'

Chapter 4

Historical Reflections on
Contemporary Antisemitism

STEVEN J. ZIPPERSTEIN

Friedrich Nietzsche observed that abstract terms are prone to overuse, as a result of which they lose all specific meaning, like old coins whose features have been worn away by excessive handling. In this essay, Steven Zipperstein urges us to define 'antisemitism' carefully, as he distinguishes the term's specific meaning – an irrational fear or hatred of Jews – from such varied phenomena as opposition to specific Israeli policies, generic anti-Americanism (in which Israel figures prominently for its intimate relationship with the United States), or even a visceral dislike of Israel based on the naive notion that in any political conflict dominance may be equated with moral culpability, and that victimization automatically instils virtue. Zipperstein also raises the issue of how past traumas, especially the Holocaust, colour Jewish perceptions of the world, which, in the Jewish collective memory, is a far crueller place than the last fifty years of rapid social mobility and integration would suggest.

* * *

Not infrequently, our most contentious, conflicted conversations we have with ourselves. This statement is not meant to be the confession of a narcissist. Rather, it is meant as an admission that even in the university world, which is, one would think, designed so that faculty, students, and others can talk genuinely and sincerely, there are some areas, often among the most sensitive, that remain simply, even persistently, somewhere beyond the pale.

I do not believe that the university is, as some have insisted, especially during the intellectual battles of the 1990s regarding the fate of the teaching of Western civilization and the like, a battleground of competing dogmas. It remains – based at least on my experience – the rare, precious setting where ideas are, on the whole, the prime, central commodity, where intellectual acuity, not orthodoxy, is the stated, explicit goal. Still, there are, not surprisingly, critically important things that remain unsaid there too. Some things feel too painful, too confounding, to speak about with coherence or precision, too raw to inspire more than the most tentative, preliminary statements.

This, no doubt, is a by-product of the isolation of intellectual and academic life. We sit mostly alone as writers and academics in the humanities, and the yearning for community and concurrence and the disinclination to isolate oneself, especially from the more socially or politically engaged of our students or colleagues, are vivid, palpable influences. In the academic circles with which I am most familiar, equivocation regarding abortion rights or U.S. Supreme Court Justice Clarence Thomas's loathsome credentials for the bench immediately cuts off communication. (As it happens, these are issues about which I agree with my peers.) But, as is increasingly clear, a belief in the State of Israel's culpability for essentially all that has gone wrong in Israel and Palestine is part and parcel of accepted opinion. Increasingly, it is deemed part of what a reasonably informed, progressive, decent person thinks.

To be sure, I live in the San Francisco Bay area, where trends are, if anything, precipitous; nevertheless, its function as a bellwether for American left-leaning opinion over the last several decades has remained constant and reliable. That Israel might be written off by, in effect, much of the left and, perhaps, even by a substantial number of liberal opinion-makers in the Western world as this decade's South Africa – what this means, especially when seen against the backdrop of attitudes towards Jews in modernity – is the concern at the heart of this paper.

Antisemitism has few respectable defenders remaining in the Western world today. As an explicit, pronounced ideology, it remains still a relic of a wretched past, the plaything of lunatics and rogues. What exists now, some assert, is a new twist on old, discredited themes. As Harvard president Lawrence Summers has argued, there is now a widespread current of opinion that encourages, as he puts it, a functional antisemitism marked by disproportionate preoccupation with Jews and the Jewish state. Irrespective of motive, it results in actions or attitudes that are themselves biased.[1]

What I explore in this paper, from the vantage point of a modern Jewish historian, is how one might understand better this recent, intense preoccupation with Jews, and especially with Israel. What relationship is there between such phenomena and what historian Robert Wistrich has dubbed the 'longest hatred'? Are they, in effect, one and the same? If so, how do they draw on one another? If not, what gives birth to and sustains these new and, in some quarters, fierce preoccupations?

It is, as I see it, the primary task of intellectuals to ask deep, probing, nettling questions, to raise problems that unsettle or exasperate. And while I do not scant the importance of clear-cut, definitive answers, I offer you few. I trust that this paper's open-ended grappling with sensitive, even painful, issues will not frustrate readers, but rather will provoke reflection and help them grapple with these issues themselves.

* * *

'Superstition,' the distinguished talmudist Saul Lieberman allegedly declared (there are several variants of this quotation), 'is nonsense, but the study of superstition is scholarship.' No one who has followed even in a cursory fashion modern antisemitic literature – its etiology, its themes, and its preoccupations – could better capture the spirit of this aphorism. Nothing is quite so repetitive, so illogical, so downright silly as antisemitic literature. Yet, as must now be clear, to refer still to such literature as silly is to dismiss its obvious, abiding resonance, its power, its ability to survive long after nearly all reasonable people have declared its dearest aspirations dead and its voice, beyond its most immediate coterie, inaudible.

'Unprovoked, irrational hostility' is the definition of antisemitism posited by one recent synthetic study.[2] It is precisely the interplay between irrational and rational hostility that is among the more salient, persistent themes in secondary literature on the subject – a theme that has, of course, been given new, even startling vitality in the wake of the 11 September 2001 attacks against the United States and the new, increasingly severe scrutiny of Jews, and especially of the Jewish state, that followed in its wake.

The fullest argument, it seems to me, for the necessity to distinguish between rational and irrational, or what some call baseless, anti-Jewishness – between hatred of Jews with and without at least some concrete foundation in terms of Jewish life or faith – is elaborated in the work of my Stanford colleague Gavin Langmuir, especially in his book *Toward a Definition of Antisemitism*. (One is reminded while perusing this book of the coy but intriguing definition of antisemitism as describing the sentiments of someone who hates Jews more than is absolutely necessary.) As Langmuir sees it, the origins of antisemitism – which he understands as the boundless, groundless hatred of Jews – may be traced only to the late Middle Ages. At that time, for complex reasons including growing, widespread doubt about the veracity of Christian faith, there ensued a militant persecution of Jews and Christian heretics that far transcended the long-standing rational – although, to be sure, politically and demographically unequal – competition of previous eras between the two monotheistic faiths. Anti-Judaism now descended into heinous fantasy, and the prospects for accusations, absurd but somehow emotionally reassuring, of systematic Jewish use of Christian blood were played out against the backdrop of the Black Death, mounting religious doubts, and a desperate search for a semblance of certainty. Now, writes Langmuir,

'the Jews' became the symbol of the fundamental and much more complex problem of unbelief in general. The various expressions of the concept of the Jewish Christ-killers identified the fundamental menace – that Christ might only be a dead human and that Christian belief was lifeless. And through that xenophobic assertion or expression of alarm, not only was awareness of that most frightening menace repressed, but as accusation the charge enabled many Christians through many centuries to release their tensions or repress their own doubts by attacking Jews.[3]

Langmuir's chronology has been vigorously criticized. Some historians have found evidence of far more than episodic, idiosyncratic, even ferocious anti-Judaism in Greek and Roman society before the rise of Christianity, let alone its late-medieval furies; others have suggested that his dating of antisemitism to pre-modern times is itself anachronistic, that it superimposes a phenomenon born of the singular frustrations, the excruciating, distinctly modern exasperations of the late nineteenth century and later onto earlier times. The interplay between rational and irrational sentiments, others argue, is less stark than Langmuir asserts; the bases for irrational reactions against Jews were firmer even in ancient times than his framework allows. Still, Langmuir's work remains justly influential in its insistence on the distinction between a rationally inspired 'anti-Judaism' – born of real, tangible religious conflict – and the attack on an entire people's ostensibly intrinsic, heinous characteristics that is, as he sees it, the most reliable, working definition for antisemitism.

'Hating Jews more than is absolutely necessary' – I characterized the phrase above as coy, as indeed it is. I return to it now because, as a definition, it provides an uncannily useful perspective on a very recent, jarring, but unavoidable phenomenon: the rise of a present-day intense preoccupation with Jews, and especially its nexus with a new, suddenly intense preoccupation with Israel. In order to speak about these preoccupations, I offer the following three caveats:

1 Criticism of Israeli policy cannot be seen, clearly, as synonymous with anti-Zionism, let alone antisemitism. Israeli public opinion is itself, needless to say, profoundly divided over the central issues concerning peace and war with the Palestinians; in a recent Israeli Supreme Court decision regarding

whether Israeli soldiers can claim the status of conscientious objector in their refusal to serve in the West Bank and Gaza, the decision cited, explicitly, the fractious, divisive nature of the Israeli polity with regard to Palestinian policy as a prime reason to turn down the soldiers' petition. It reminded the petitioners that it was not inconceivable that soldiers might be told in the future (as they were in the wake of Israel's 1979 peace treaty with Egypt) to remove Jewish settlers, and then soldiers hostile to this policy could, in turn, object to following these orders. Israel is deeply divided over its relationship, now and in the future, with the Palestinians, and there is no reason why Jews or others elsewhere should not be expected to weigh in, should not be expected to care about and debate these matters that have an impact on the world's security, on the fate of lands deemed holy by all the West's major faiths, and on an issue with significant, complex moral implications.

2 Antisemitism, for Jews of my generation in the United States, born as we were after the implosion of school quotas, after the restrictions on employment and clubs and neighbourhoods of the past, has been until very recently little more than a faded memory, remote, almost mute. (I describe here conditions in the United States, to be sure, not Canada.) The only first-hand encounter – an undeniably tepid one – that I, as a child born and raised in a large urban centre (Los Angeles), have ever had with antisemitism was when, as a university student in the 1970s, I was waiting to pay for my meal at a coffee shop while the cashier, a young woman in her twenties, counted the money paid by the previous customer who had just left and declared aloud, 'That fellow Jewed me.' I was amazed and furious. I had never before heard that expression uttered by anyone. I asked her if she knew what she had said and repeated the phrase to her. I told her that, as a Jew, I found the statement deplorable. She looked puzzled. For her, perhaps, it was no more than a phrase with the dimmest of implications. And that is where the encounter – and, indeed, my personal, concrete association with antisemitism of any sort, in the United States at least – begins and ends. My own happily, ridiculously pampered generation, as *New Republic* literary editor Leon Wieseltier put it recently, are 'the luckiest Jews who ever lived. We are even the spoiled brats of Jewish history.' 'Jewish history,' he proposes, 'now consists essentially in a competition between Israel and the United States, between the blandishments of sovereignty and the blandishments of pluralism; it is a friendly competition, and by the standards of the Jewish experience it is an embarrassment of riches.'[4] And there remains ample evidence that antisemitism in the United States is an ever-remote passion, something that barely resonates even as a historical

memory. Take as an example the transformation of the hit movie *About Schmidt*, starring Jack Nicholson, which originated as a Louis Begley novel about a dour WASP lawyer opposed to his daughter's prospective marriage to a young Jewish law partner. The filmmakers concluded, it seems, that moviegoers simply would not understand why anyone would so deeply object to the marriage of their daughter to a Jewish lawyer, and so they transmuted the son-in-law into a waterbed salesman – apparently an occupation so noisome or absurd as to inspire general disdain. A romantic relationship with a Jew simply did not. In a more serious vein, Joseph Lieberman's candidacy in 2000 for the U.S. vice-presidency, the primary campaign of Pennsylvania senator Arlen Specter, the recent candidacy of Lieberman for the 2004 Democratic nomination – none have inspired much anti-Jewish response. 'The spoiled brats of Jewish history,' indeed.

3 Still, over the course of these singularly sanguine decades (by Jewish standards, at least) since the 1950s and 1960s, it remains clear that for many American Jews – as judged on the basis of surveys, anecdotal evidence, or the focus of Jewish communal campaigns – antisemitism has remained a real threat, an often acute source of concern, for some even the true, dark reality lurking beneath an ever-deceptively safe, secure public life. Many students of Jewish public life have commented over the years on what seems to have been the curious, puzzling, even unsettling discrepancy between the objective safety and the subjective unease felt by so many American Jews. The nexus in post-1960s America between minority status and victimization, the rapid interplay between the devastation of the Holocaust and the rise of Israel, the startling, understandable unreality implicit in the assertion that America, quite simply, is a different place, basically a better place for Jews, and, finally, the sheer efficacy, the raw, undiminished power of antisemitism as a communal rallying call – all these, no doubt, have played a role.

*   *   *

Let us proceed towards the main point. 'We shall never fully understand anti-Semitism,' writes David Berger, a scholar of medieval Jewish history. 'Deep-rooted, complex, endlessly persistent, constantly changing yet remaining the same, it is a phenomenon that stands at the intersection of history, sociology, economics, political science, religion, and psychology.' He recalls a conversation he had with a Jew who confided to Berger his fears of the aftermath of a nuclear war: 'He does not fear radiation, or climatic change, or wounds crying vainly for treatment; he worries instead that the war will be blamed on Einstein,

Oppenheimer, and Teller. Macabre Jewish humor, no doubt, or simple paranoia. And yet ...'[5]

Clearly, what is at stake here is unease regarding the requirements of proportionality, an ability to sensibly assess blame, intelligently evaluate casual relationships – political, social, or otherwise – in ways born of perceptions of a real, not mythical, world. Such perceptions, clearly, can vastly differ; the lines separating an intense preoccupation from an obsession are, not infrequently, obscure. But the fact that, especially in the wake of 11 September, David Berger's anecdote is now suddenly, undeniably jarring, in ways inconceivable beforehand, should give us pause.

That Jews – and in particular the Jewish state – should loom so large, so prominently, so persistently now in talk regarding contemporary politics worldwide, that the line separating nonsense and news with regard to Jews and especially with regard to Israel is now so widely, so nakedly disregarded, cannot but startle us all. There are, to be sure, many reasons for the high visibility of the Israeli-Palestinian conflict, and by no means are all these products of mendacity, blindness, or bigotry. Jews are inescapably visible in the Western world – by virtue of their professions, their social mobility, their many successes in modernity, and, of course, their centrality in the core teachings of Christianity. (Recently, on a transcontinental flight, a woman sitting next to me – as it turns out a Stanford engineering graduate student from Italy – asked me, when she learned what I did, how many Jews still lived in Europe. She added that she assumed, having been in the United States for the last six or seven years, that about 10 per cent of the U.S. population was Jewish. And, from what I could see, she was no bigot. A complementary anecdote: Woodrow Wilson, not singularly bigoted, commented at the peace conference following the First World War, on the numbers of Jews in the world; the figure he came up with, off the top of his head, was twice the true number of Jews.) Israel's visibility, in turn, has – now and in the recent past – much to do with the power of Middle East oil, Israel's exceptionally close relationship with the United States, the singularly large amount of aid it receives annually from the United States, the freedom with which reporters can traverse it, its democratic form of government, and also with the real tragedy, the apparent intractability of the Palestinian conflict. It has, in short, much to do with real, truly difficult, even excruciatingly complicated issues.

Still, the real issue at hand is how and why a variety of factors – the implosion of the Oslo accords, the Second Intifada, the new, heightened emphasis on Palestinian suicide bombings, the fierce reactions of the Sharon government, and the reconfiguration of the post–11 September world – all contributed to what is now, over most of the globe, an overwhelmingly respectable excoriation of Israel. The assault against Israel is no longer directed merely at the policies of the state but increasingly, or so it feels at times, at the very legitimacy of its existence. Fiercely visible in the Muslim world, increasingly unabashed, it seems, elsewhere, in France, in England, even Germany, a some-times wildly unrestrained freedom on the part of even those trained in consum-mate restraint is now apparent. We now hear the most astonishingly nasty things about Israel: 'A shitty little country,' in the now-infamous, chilling, dinner-party formulation of France's ambassador to England, Daniel Bernard, in December of 2001. Also in December of 2001, the London *Spectator* wrote that 'anti-Semitism and its open expression has become respectable at London dinner parties.' Hence also the declamation by the distinguished biographer of Tolstoy, the British writer A.N. Wilson, in London's *Evening Standard* on 22 October 2001, that he had 'reluctantly' come to the conclusion, in view of Israeli treatment of Palestinians, that the Jewish state had no right to exist. In Europe, hundreds of academics, primarily in England, pressed the European Union to cease its dealings with Israeli academics (who have, as it happens, for decades been at the forefront of the Israeli peace movement) and their institu-tions as a protest against Israeli policy in the Occupied Territories.[6]

In the United States, an effort to pressure universities to divest financial holdings in Israel has ended, it would seem, in failure (no university, to the best of my knowledge, agreed to do so), and counter-petitions garnered immeasur-ably more faculty support than did the petitions favouring divestment. But in intellectual life it is rarely the majority, even within the relatively rarefied context of universities, that shapes the trajectory of debate. Those responsible for the divestment campaign may have anticipated losing in the short term, but they have managed, as I see it, to press the debate over Israel away from the sectarian margins and immeasurably closer to the centre of university political life. To occupy centre stage, as organizers of the Israel divestment campaign have made clear, remains their goal, and its achievement is not inconceivable.

Centre stage: here we come to the rub. That the Israel-Palestine debate occupies, as it has for the last half-century, centre stage in the political debates of Jews and Palestinians in the Middle East and beyond it, that it constitutes for both groups a critical litmus test for the widest range of political, even moral, concerns seems self-evident, even unavoidable. That it increasingly occupies something eerily close to centre stage in political chat on the Internet, at European dinner parties, in the cultural politics of the European Union, in the political deliberations of the left in this country and elsewhere – how can this be explained if not with reference to the uncanny resilience of antisemitism?

Some of this obsession with Israel is, no doubt, a by-product of antisemitism –

the by-product of a belief, often, to be sure, little more than a predilection to believe, that Jews are uncannily influential beyond their actual numbers and that their behaviour as individuals and also as a group tends to be disruptive or, in the minds of some, even malevolent. It is impossible to dismiss the importance, the uncanny resilience of such attitudes. Speaking, however, in terms of the preoccupations of intellectuals in the West, it seems that responses to Jews and the Jewish state are not fundamentally the byproduct of antisemitism. They are, above all, a by-product of the wildly disproportionate responses that mark the post–11 September world. Disproportionate reaction seems increasingly the norm, especially with regard to antipathy for the United States, antipathy that has meshed, it seems to me, with an outsized antagonism for its smallest but singularly visible Middle East ally, Israel. Distinguishing such reactions from antisemitism without denying that the two coincide is not meant to dismiss the significance of such attitudes, which remain troubling, but in ways different from how they have been widely understood.

Disproportionate reaction among academics and intellectuals to Israel and Zionism is by no means new. Perhaps my favorite example from the not-so-distant past is the entry on 'Zionism' in David Robertson's reference book, *The Penguin Dictionary of Politics*, published originally in 1984 and reprinted in 1993 with the following depiction, released in the immediate wake of the Oslo Agreement. Robertson is listed as a then tutor and fellow in politics at St Hugh's College, Oxford:

> Nowadays Zionism principally refers to a hawk versus dove orientation toward Israeli policy. Zionists support at least the retention of the land gained in the various Arab-Israeli wars since 1947, and possibly a further integration of these areas by settlement of Jewish immigrants mainly from the former USSR. Zionism still retains considerable support, often among financially and politically powerful Jewish lobbies in Western countries, especially in the USA. Non-Zionists, whether Jewish, Israeli, or neither, increasingly believe that some sort of accommodation, almost certainly involving the creation of a Palestinian state inside the current de facto Israeli borders, is both right and politically necessary.[7]

Among other things, this definition of non-Zionism, as Robertson puts it in the 1993 edition of his reference work, would include Israel's prime minister at the time, Yitzhak Rabin, much of his cabinet, the Labour party, nearly all of the Kibbutz movement, and, arguably, the bulk of the population of Tel Aviv and Haifa. Still, there is no reason to think of Robertson – woefully ignorant of the most elementary facts in Zionist history (note that in his definition Zionists are those who support 'the retention of land gained in the various

Arab-Israeli wars since 1947') – as an antisemite. Nor is his opposition predicated, it would seem, on much thought, or insight, or, for that matter, a sustained interest in Zionism.

Attitudes like those of Robertson are now immeasurably more widespread; arguably, in some quarters they are normative. It is a mistake, in this respect, not to distinguish, as has the respected social analyst Earl Raab (long head of the Jewish Community Relations Commission of San Francisco) in a soon-to-be-published essay, between what he calls anti-Israelism and antisemitism. These manifestations are not, he argues, necessarily the same. What Raab means by anti-Israelism is the increasing role that a concerted, vigorous prejudice against Israel – and he does see such sentiments as born of prejudice – has played in much of the political left, visibly in the antiglobalist campaign, but where there is no discernible hatred of Jews. Often in this context, belief in Israel's mendacity is shaped, above all, by simple, crude, linear notions of the casual relationship between politics, oppression, and liberation, by transparent beliefs in a world with clear-cut oppressors and oppressed – in other words, by a much distorted, simplistic, but this-worldly political analysis devoid of anti-Jewish bias.[8]

Such prejudice against Israel is not the same as antisemitism, although undoubtedly the two can and at times do coexist. Nor should it be confused with criticism of Israel – a society that is now, more than ever, deeply, profoundly fractured and where self-criticism is rife. It is, rather, born of a distinct prejudice, not infrequently a Manichean view of politics, a tendency to draw neat and superficial divisions between good and bad in public affairs. Still, however unsettling and wrong-headed this sort of anti-Israeli sentiment may be, it is predicated on real, concrete perceptions, typically with little if any connection to an antagonism towards Jews.

Not only bigots or fools, not only the ignorant or the insensitive, might well be unsettled and unsure how to respond with requisite intelligence or empathy to the contemporary history of a people who, within the span of little more than half a century, were subjected to systematic murder in Europe, all but wiped out in much of the continent, and who, within the blink of an eye, it sometimes seems, became masters of their own state, negotiating partners with great powers, a pillar of U.S. foreign policy, a formidable regional force. This proximity startles Jews, too; we find it difficult, at times, to acknowledge the basic, obvious, inescapable stability of our lives, the relative absence of strife or hatred of a sort that was, so recently, so normative and that dissipated, in so much of the Western world and beyond it too, so quickly.

Consequently, we are prone at times to see unease as normative, to see ease as a respite, even a delusion; we are prone to see a Jewish state as, perhaps, more vulnerable, less powerful, less culpable, as victim and not as an actor, at least partly because – so very recently in our own history – we were the quintessential victims. We were mostly undefended and overwhelmingly friendless, and this trauma continues to haunt and perhaps at times to distort our sense of the world around us now. When we encounter antagonism – especially outsized, disproportionate antagonism – the memories of horrible times, whether personally experienced or imbibed secondhand, elicit reactions that are often sincere, acute, and disorienting.

How to determine where prejudice ends and antisemitic bigotry begins – how to determine the difference between politics and metaphysics, between protest, however excessive, and unvarnished hatred – is, of course, excruciatingly difficult. Perceptions can – and perceptions often do, as Jews know perhaps better than most – have a life of their own, one that must be taken deadly seriously. At the same time, one must, in the life of a healthy person as in the existence of a healthy people, distinguish between perceptions predicated on fact and those shaped by myth. Facts themselves, of course, can tell such different, conflicting tales, and never more so, it seems, than in the history of the Israeli state. As Derek Penslar wrote recently in *Sh'ma* magazine,

> Theodor Herzl wrote that world Jewry had the financial power to save the bankrupt Ottoman Empire. That is a fact. It's also a fact that Herzl was wrong, but he may have truly believed it. It is a fact that by the summer of 1948 Israel enjoyed military superiority over the Arabs – but the Israelis didn't know it. It is equally correct to claim that the Israeli military entered the 1967 war confident of victory or gripped by existential panic. And so on, up to the present, where one of the most powerful nations on earth is also among the most fragile.[9]

NOTES

1 'Serious and thoughtful people are advocating and taking actions that are anti-Semitic in their effect if not their intent.' Quoted from Lawrence Summers's 'Address at Morning Prayers,' Memorial Church, Cambridge, MA, 17 September 2002.
2 Milton Shain, *Antisemitism* (London: Bowerdean, 1998), 5.
3 Gavin Langmuir, *Toward a Definition of Antisemitism* (Berkeley, CA: University of California Press, 1990), 333.
4 Leon Wieseltier, 'Hitler Is Dead,' *New Republic*, 16 May 2002.
5 David Berger, *History and Hate: The Dimensions of Anti-Semitism* (Philadelphia: Jewish Publication Society, 1986), 3, 14.

6 See Hillel Halkin, 'The Return of Anti-Semitism,' *Commentary* (February 2002).
7 David Robertson, *The Penguin Dictionary of Politics*, 2nd ed. (London: Penguin Books, 1993), 494.
8 Typescript provided by the author: 'Prejudice against Israel and the New Anti-Semitism.'
9 Derek Penslar, 'Teaching Israeli History: The Unbearable Heaviness of Jewish Power,' *Sh'ma* (December 2002): 7.

Chapter 5

Antisemitism in Western Europe Today

TODD M. ENDELMAN

In the chapter that follows, Professor Todd Endelman challenges the widely held notion that contemporary antisemitism in Western Europe harks back to the anti-Jewish crises of the 1930s. People of goodwill regularly urge us to think this way. And, to be sure, there is some evidence, reported here, of the persistence of antisemitic myths in countries that were once the feeding grounds of the Holocaust. However, that is by no means the end of the story. Informed by a careful reading of the historical past as well as present-day conditions, Endelman highlights the way in which West European anti-Jewish mobilization springs from a post-Holocaust political culture, an anti-American and pro–Third World orientation of the left, demographic changes in European society, and the heightened level of conflict in the Middle East. How dangerous is the present situation? Endelman urges us to keep matters in perspective. 'On balance,' he writes, 'the new antisemitism is worrisome but not yet threatening.' Analysts have a responsibility to make distinctions, remain faithful to the evidence, and be on the lookout for what is new. This essay admirably does all three.

* * *

George Santayana's dictum that 'those who cannot remember the past are condemned to repeat it' is misleading and even dangerous advice. Its message – know the errors of your predecessors so you do not repeat them – fosters the illusion that history repeats itself in easily comprehensible ways and that those who are alert to this are prepared to face the future. It errs in assuming that seemingly similar events across decades and centuries are in their essentials identical regardless of the circumstances in which they are found. It ignores the possibility that the newest manifestations of a phenomenon may be both similar and dissimilar simultaneously and thus require a fundamental reassessment and altogether different response than earlier manifestations.

West European statesmen learned this the hard way in the 1930s. Shattered by the toll in human life that the First World War took, they struggled in the decade before the Second World War to avoid another large-scale bloodletting. In pursuit of peace at any cost, they worked to appease Adolf Hitler and his regime – only to become engulfed in an even more horrific, apocalyptic conflict within a few years. The Jews of Germany also thought they knew the lessons of history and that they would be able to outlast a regime that would either moderate its racial views or pass from the scene, as had earlier anti-Jewish regimes. Only after *Kristallnacht* destroyed the illusion that a Jewish community could survive in Germany did the majority of them recognize that Nazi antisemitism was qualitatively different from Wilhelminian antisemitism. Only then did the majority scramble to find refuge abroad – at which point escape was difficult and often impossible. In North America as well, Jews filtered news of the war years through the lens of history. When reports of mass shootings on the eastern front reached them, many initially believed that the massacres were another chapter in the long history of pogroms in that part of the world. But, as we now know, the systematic killings of the *Einsatzgruppen* heralded something altogether new.

Just as consciousness of the past shaped how Jews and Gentiles responded to the rise of Nazism and the Holocaust, so too consciousness of these events in turn has shaped understandings of and responses to current outbreaks of anti-Jewish hostility. The destruction of the bulk of European Jewry during the war and the inability of Western Jews to do much to prevent it has heightened contemporary Jewish attentiveness to antisemitism. Levels of hostility and stigmatization to which Jews in the first half of the twentieth century were resigned now appear intolerable in the eyes of their children and grandchildren. It is difficult for them to regard antisemitism as simply a social inconvenience or an affront to their self-esteem. The Holocaust has left them nervous and on edge, sensitive to the potential consequences of widespread Jew-baiting, to the linkage between words and deeds. However, if memories of the Holocaust have made them vigilant, they may also have imposed a framework on the way in which they interpret current events that distorts the meaning of those events. If we are to understand the latest currents of Jew-baiting, then we must clearly grasp how they are both similar and dissimilar to their predecessors.

That there is more hostility to Jews in Western Europe now than there was a decade or two earlier is widely accepted. While I cannot undertake a full review of the evidence, I do want to highlight the ways in which this hostility manifests itself. The most visibly shocking way is an outbreak of violence against Jewish property and persons. In Belgium, France, and Britain, a score of synagogues have been attacked or ransacked since the beginning of the new millennium. The most dramatic incidents have occurred in France. On

3 October 2000, arsonists all but destroyed the synagogue of Villepinte in north-eastern suburban Paris. Within the next ten days, four more synagogues, all in greater Paris, were burned. That month, in France as a whole, another two dozen incidents of attempted arson were reported. In spring 2002, antisemites in Lyons smashed the doors of a synagogue and community centre, using a car equipped with battering rams; in Marseilles, they burnt a synagogue to the ground and in Toulouse opened fire on a kosher butcher shop. Jewish students have been harassed in the public schools; Jewish worshippers on their way to synagogue have been assaulted; school buses with Jewish students have been stoned. CRIF, the umbrella organization of French Jewry, recorded 500 anti-Jewish incidents from early September 2000 through early April 2002. One indication of how far tolerance has deteriorated is that the number of Jews who left France to settle in Israel in 2001 (2,556) was double the number in the previous year and the most since 1967.[1] Elsewhere in Western Europe, the number of violent incidents has escalated, along similar lines but not in the dramatic way it has in France.

Throughout Western Europe, verbal violence has escalated as well. Along-side the taunts of hooligans and skinheads and the ravings of Holocaust deniers and neo-Nazis, expressions of overt hostility have sprouted in the liberal media. The cover of the London weekly *New Statesman* (14 January 2002), long the flagship journal of the British left, carried the headline 'A Kosher Conspiracy?' and featured a gold Magen David piercing a Union Jack. The story claimed to describe the influence of a rich, potent Zionist lobby that harassed, threatened, and smeared journalists who did not toe 'the Jewish line' on Israel. (Given the scathing criticism of Israel in much of the British press, as well as by the British Broadcasting Corporation, it would seem that this Jewish lobby is much less powerful and effective than its critics imagine it to be.) Even left-wing Jewish journalists who had been sceptical of Anglo-Jewish complaints about antisemitism were unable to remain quiet. *Guardian* columnist Jonathan Freedland wrote, 'The message could not have been plainer: wealthy Jews were plotting to subordinate a defenceless, overwhelmed Britain ... [The cover] would not have looked out of place in *Der Stürmer* ... It was an image replete with almost classic antisemitism: rich Jews dominating their besieged host country.'[2] *Independent* columnist Stephen Pollard wrote in equally impassioned terms that he was convinced that 'antisemitism is now acceptable again in polite society.' He came to this sobering realization after a dinner party at which one guest told him she was boycotting Jewish businesses because of Israel's treatment of the Palestinians. When he challenged her, another guest interjected, 'Don't get at her. She's only saying out loud what we all think: the Jews need to be taught that, terrible as the Holocaust was, you can't rely on that excuse forever – and certainly not to justify what you are doing to the Palestinians.'[3] The liberal Italian daily *La Stampa* even revived the hoary charge of deicide: a cartoon showing the baby Jesus in the manger looking at an Israeli tank carried the caption 'Don't tell me they want to kill me again.' In the same vein, a bishop in Copenhagen, in a Sunday sermon, likened Ariel Sharon to King Herod, who ordered the murder of all male children in Bethlehem under the age of two.[4] In short, the *bien pensant* chattering classes experience no compunction, as they might once have done, about deploying classic anti-Jewish tropes.

When we turn from elite opinion to public opinion, the task of assessment becomes more difficult. Survey research is a flawed art, at best. The willingness of interviewees to reveal to pollsters their opinions is different from their willingness and ability to act in support of these opinions. In other words, opinions are one matter; deeds, another. Moreover, the manner in which the researcher poses a question – the words and phrases he or she uses – influences the responses he or she receives. Nonetheless, for want of any other alternative, public opinion research will have to suffice. The picture that emerges from various polls is not encouraging. From 1988 to 1991, 20 per cent of French citizens thought that 'Jews have too much power.' In 1999, the proportion rose to 31 per cent; in 2000, to 34 per cent.[5] An Anti-Defamation League-sponsored survey of attitudes regarding Jews in five European states (Spain, Italy, Switzerland, Austria, and the Netherlands), the results of which were announced in fall 2002, discovered that 27 per cent of the population believe that 'Jews are more likely than others to use shady practices to get what they want' and that 60 per cent believe that 'Jews are more loyal to Israel than this country.'[6] In Italy, a country not known for its animosity to Jews, views of Jews have also become more critical. A poll conducted by the newspaper *Corriere della Sera* found that in 2001 23 per cent of those interviewed believed that Jews were unpleasant and not to be trusted (in comparison to 14 per cent in 2000) and that 44 per cent believed that Jews should stop presenting themselves as victims of the Holocaust (in comparison to 35 per cent the year before).[7]

The resurgence of anti-Jewish violence and views in Western Europe in recent years is disturbing, but whether it presents the same kind of threat to Jews that pre-war antisemitism did requires further comment. If we compare recent hostility to the antisemitism that flourished between 1870 and 1939, critical differences emerge. (By this, I do not want to suggest that recent manifestations are not threatening, but rather that their threat is of a different order and a different magnitude.) Here, then, are some major differences between today's hostility to Jews in Western Europe and the antisemitism of the half-century before Hitler.

First, no contemporary West European political party with parliamentary representation seeks to reverse the process of Jewish emancipation – that is, to strip Jews of their citizenship and reclassify them as aliens or to restrict their participation in state, society, and culture and return them to the margins of national life. This was the central objective of political antisemitism before the Second World War. The illiberal, hierarchical, antimeritocratic politics of most conservative parties led them to oppose the unfettered participation of Jews in economic and cultural life. This kind of political antisemitism no longer stalks the parliamentary chambers of Western Europe or the drawing rooms of the rich and the well bred. Another way of saying this is that the 'Jewish Question,' as it existed before the Second World War, is no longer a central or even a peripheral issue in West European politics. At the start of the twenty-first century, bashing immigrants or Americans is a much more effective election-eering strategy than bashing Jews.

Second, antisemitism in Western Europe is no longer intimately linked to a set of mutually reinforcing antiliberal beliefs. Before the Second World War, antisemitism was, in Shulamit Volkov's felicitous phrase, a cultural code.[8] It stood for, drew energy from, and in turn strengthened a radical antimodern mentality that included opposition to unfettered capitalism, urbanization, industrialization, secularization, democracy, parliamentary politics, social mobility, meritocracy, cultural modernism, and feminism. In the second half of the twentieth century, antisemitism became detached (although not completely) from this bundle of antimodernist discontent and hence lost much of its imaginative and political power, at least in the West. (In the lands of Islam, of course, antimodernist antisemitism still rages.)

Third, antisemitism no longer hinders Jewish social or economic mobility. In the nineteenth century and the first half of the twentieth century, social prejudice and occupational discrimination embittered the lives of several gen-erations of talented, ambitious Jews. Tens of thousands converted to Christian-ity or legally withdrew from their communities (in the cases of Germany and Austria). Even more of them, their ambition and hope thwarted, lived with their anger and resentment, some of which they mistakenly redirected towards their own ethnic background (which they saw as the principal cause of their misfortune). Barriers to Jewish integration remained strong through the 1950s but after that began to weaken. In contemporary Britain and France, educated, middle-class Jews, those Jews who felt the weight of discrimination most cruelly earlier, are professionally successful, socially integrated, and well repre-sented in political life. In Britain, in the days of Margaret Thatcher and John Major, Jews held high political office, including such top posts as chancellor of the exchequer and secretary for defence, foreign, and home affairs. In Western

Europe, being Jewish is no longer an obstacle to social acceptance, economic mobility, and political prominence.

Fourth, antisemitism no longer benefits from the political instability and extremism that plagued Europe in the interwar period and nourished conspiratorial and delusional thinking about Jews. Since the end of the Second World War, Western Europe has enjoyed remarkable political stability and economic prosperity. The forces of the left and the right no longer face each other in battle formation, threatening revolution and upheaval. Instead, the universal franchise, the parliamentary system, the mixed economy, and the social welfare net enjoy broad popular support. Pragmatism has overtaken (although not vanquished) extremism. Those political groups that want to subvert the status quo and remake state and society, whether in a reactionary or a revolutionary direction, are very much on the margins of politics.

Fifth, before the Second World War, the right, rather than the left, was the paramount source of hatred and contempt for European Jews. Historically, liberalism promoted legal emancipation and social integration, the free movement of persons and property, while conservatism stood for the maintenance of the old regime, with its ranks, corporations, and restrictive practices. At the turn of the century, it was the left, not the right, that in France came to Dreyfus's defence and in Britain fought immigration restrictions. In Germany and Austria, the ferocity and omnipresence of antisemitism everywhere on the right guaranteed that Jews would find a political home on the left – whether among liberals, social democrats, or communists. This is no longer true. On the right, antisemitism no longer functions as a rallying cry, while on the left it has become entangled with and draws support from political currents that were non-existent or unimportant before the Second World War – specifically, anti-Americanism, Third Worldism, and antiglobalism – a linkage to which I will return further on.

Sixth, alongside left-wing parties and movements, there is another new fount of hostility to Jews in Western Europe – Islam – that was altogether absent in earlier periods. There are between 15 and 25 million Muslims in Europe as a whole, not all of whom, of course, identify with radical Islam and its anti-Jewish agenda. In France alone, Muslims number about 6 million – or 10 per cent of the population. These communities stem from Europe's former overseas colonies (as well as Turkey) and are still growing, through both a high natural birth rate and largely illegal immigration. On the whole, they are more separatist than integrationist in their stance towards the societies in which they have settled (although this may change in the future), and in socio-economic terms constitute a distinct underclass, with all that that implies in terms of poverty, crime, unemployment, alienation, and poor schooling. Given the crude, unreconstructed Jew-baiting of the societies from which they stem, where the blood libel, for example, is a daily staple, it is not surprising that Muslims in Europe have reactivated forms of anti-Jewish behaviour that were once the preserve of fascists and pogromists. The spread of a highly politicized radical Islam has only aggravated this hatred of Jews. In France, where anti-Jewish violence is most marked, Muslim youth, the children of parents who emigrated from North Africa in the 1960s and 1970s, have perpetrated most of the attacks on Jewish buildings and persons. But the problem extends beyond the small number of disaffected youth who resort to violence. As a French political scientist remarked, 'What is an average French teacher to do when 70 per cent of the class object to a course in religious tolerance giving Judaism its proper due or simply refuse to attend a discussion about the Holocaust on the grounds that it is a Zionist lie? More often than not, he or she drops the matter altogether.'[9] In many French schools, in fact, administrators have cancelled Holocaust-awareness programs because of opposition from Muslim students. By late February 2003, anti-Jewish violence and harassment were so marked in schools with large Muslim populations that the minister of education, Luc Ferry, felt compelled to introduce anti-incitement measures.[10] His intervention broke two politically correct taboos: it acknowledged that France's Muslim community is a source of racist violence and that left-wing teachers tolerate such behaviour, either because they feel guilty about France's colonial past or because they loathe Ariel Sharon – or both.

Seventh, and last, the most common and animated expressions of antisemitism in Western Europe are linked to anti-Zionism. This, too, is novel, first, because the State of Israel did not exist before the Second World War, and second, because pre-war antisemites, to the extent that they took an interest in internal Jewish politics, were often enthusiastic Zionists since a Jewish exodus from Europe was something they devoutly desired. The real novelty, however, is the lively intertwining of traditional anti-Jewish tropes and motifs with European anxieties about the rise of American power and the emergence of Jewish sovereignty.

This intertwining raises the vexed question of the extent to which current expressions of anti-Zionism are, at heart, expressions of antisemitism. Has impassioned criticism of Israeli policy become the acceptable face of antisemitism, a tolerated vehicle for venting hostility to Jews? One's response to this question depends largely on one's definition of anti-Zionism. Classifying all public criticism of the policies of Ariel Sharon as anti-Zionist – and thus antisemitic – is undoubtedly unjustified, for it equates dissent from the Likud program with intolerance and fear of Jews. A more sensible rule of thumb, it seems to me, is to ask when and under what circumstances anti-Zionism shades into antisemitism

– when it becomes something more than criticism of Israeli policy. From this perspective, I would argue that anti-Zionism crosses the line in the following instances:

1 when it questions the legitimacy of the Jewish state, but no other state, and the legitimacy of Jewish nationalism, but no other nationalism, either in the Middle East or elsewhere;
2 when it denies to the Jewish state, but no other state, the right to express the character of the majority of its citizens (that is, to be as Jewish as France is French);
3 when it demonizes the Jewish state, turning the Arab-Israeli conflict into a morality play, a problem that Jews, and Jews alone, created and for which Jews, and Jews alone, are responsible;
4 when it expresses an obsessive, exclusive, and disproportionate concern with the shortcomings of the Israelis and the sufferings of the Palestinians – to the point that a conflict between two small peoples is transformed into a cosmic, Manichean struggle between the forces of good and evil.[11]

When criticism of Israel crosses any of these lines and begins to traffic in the fantasies, obsessions, fears, and irrationalities that are the stock-in-trade of full-blown antisemitism, it becomes nearly indistinguishable from that which it claims not to be.

By this standard, the recent explosion of anti-Israel invective includes a disturbing subtext. In Western Europe, critics repeatedly invoke the old anti-Jewish, Soviet-created canard, launched in the wake of Israel's extraordinary victory over the Soviet Union's hapless Arab clients in 1967, that Israel is Nazi Germany reincarnate, that Zionism is fascism, racism, and colonialism, that Israel's occupation of the West Bank and Gaza is genocidal in practice and intent, and that its citizen-soldiers behave like SS men. This kind of inflammatory language, with its equation of Jews with the twentieth century's most vile regime, is a dead giveaway that more than a humanitarian concern about Palestinian suffering is at work. After all, there is far more human suffering in sub-Saharan Africa, where millions of lives are at risk – from civil wars, AIDS, corruption, and misgovernment – than there is in the West Bank and Gaza. Moreover, it is not difficult to identify other states, in the Middle East and beyond, that occupy territory that others claim as their national patrimony – including Syria, Iran, Iraq, Turkey, India, China, Spain, Italy, Russia, and the United States. Why, one wonders, are European statesmen, intellectuals, media personalities, and the like, obsessed with Israel's occupation of the West Bank and Gaza but, by comparison, relatively indifferent to Syria's occupation of

Lebanon, China's occupation of Tibet, Spain's occupation of Basque territory, Turkey's occupation of Kurdish territory, India's occupation of Muslim Kashmir, and Russia's occupation of Muslim lands in Central Asia? Why does the Belgian judicial system seek to prosecute Ariel Sharon, who failed to intervene when Christians murdered Muslims at Sabra and Shatila in September 1982, but takes no steps to prosecute the commander of the Dutch NATO contingent that pulled out of the Bosnian town of Srebrenica in December 1995, leaving the town's Muslims, whom the Dutch were supposed to protect, to the mercy of the Bosnians, who then massacred thousands of them? Indeed, why is there no West European judicial campaign to prosecute the Christian commanders who ordered and directed the massacres at Sabra and Shatila? When Europeans act arbitrarily and judge unequally, with one standard for the Jewish state and one standard for the rest of world, there is more than a whiff of antisemitism in the air. As Thomas Friedman noted in the weeks before the start of the war against Iraq, 'There is only one group of Arabs for whom Europeans have consistently spoken out in favor of their liberation – and that is those Arabs living under Israeli occupation, the Palestinians.'[12] When the only Arabs who are of moral interest to Europeans are those in conflict with Jews, the unavoidable conclusion is that Europeans are more interested in trashing Jews than in succouring Arabs.

Those who argue in this vein are often accused of undue anxiety – of seeing antisemites everywhere – or of rhetorical chicanery – of delegitimizing all criticism of Israeli policy by tarring it with the label of antisemitism. Supporters of Ariel Sharon, who in general are reluctant to acknowledge the harsh realities of Israel's occupation of the West Bank and Gaza and the legitimacy of Palestinian national aspirations, invite this accusation by their reluctance. Moreover, the casual, immoderate way in which they toss about the charge of antisemitism works to undermine the arguments of those who seek to delineate carefully when opposition to Israeli policy shades into Jew-baiting. Those who cry wolf all the time impede and discredit the work of those who cry wolf only when the wolf actually threatens.

At the same time, those critics who are accused of antisemitism vigorously deny it, especially those on the left, who think of themselves as broadminded, correct-thinking, progressive persons. They hotly deny that they are prejudiced, pointing out that Jews hold similar views, that they include Jews among their friends, and that they have always championed what is just. All of this may be true, but one can hold to a double standard without being conscious of it. In fact, it is in the very nature of a double standard that it remains unacknowledged. The fact that overt antisemitism is taboo in respectable society in post-Holocaust Europe (or at least has been hitherto) means that hostility to Jews will of necessity be expressed in ways that do not directly transgress the taboo.

If one accepts the conclusion that hostility to Jews has become intertwined with hostility to the State of Israel and that hostility to the State of Israel has become a respectable obsession in Western Europe, the next question is 'why?' More than a half-century after the murder of two-thirds of Europe's Jews, why have expressions of hostility to Jews once again become permissible? As with pre-war antisemitism, there is no single explanation, but rather a complex of causes, which, working in tandem, produce the heightened hostility that is often called the 'new' antisemitism.

The starting point for any analysis of the newest wave of anti-Jewish hostility is the legacy of pre-war antisemitism, both secular and religious. Although revulsion against Nazism and sympathy for its victims tended to muzzle overt expressions of antisemitism in the public sphere in the decades after the war, they did not succeed in completely uprooting centuries-old ways of thinking and feeling about Jews. Although discredited for the moment, anti-Jewish sentiments remained embedded, whether strongly or weakly is a matter of debate, in the high and low culture of Europe, in its patterns of thinking, speaking, and feeling. They continued – and still continue – to reside there, and when circumstances conspire to awaken them, they spring to life and once again play an active role in popular and elite discourse.

In a general way, this point reproduces the classic, late-nineteenth-century Zionist understanding that antisemitism was ubiquitous, eternal, and ineradicable, that no change in Jewish behaviour, including conversion to Christianity, would cause it to disappear. Whether or not the early ideologists of Zionism were correct, they failed to explain *why* this was so. They rarely entered into the question of antisemitism's extraordinary staying power.[13] Some invoked metaphors of illness and disease, but metaphors are descriptive and rhetorical devices not explanations. In any case, they were more concerned with exposing the failure of emancipation and Jewish programs of self-transformation and regeneration. At the same time, despite their inability to explain antisemitism's persistence, they believed, nonetheless, that the eventual establishment of a Jewish state would eliminate antisemitism, both because the Jews would shed their abnormality and become a people like other peoples (*ke-khol ha-goyyim*) and because the diaspora would cease to exist as Jews exited Europe and returned to their homeland. Without Jews in their midst, they reasoned, the peoples of Europe would cease to fear and hate them.

A century later it is clear that these assumptions were wrong. The reason, I believe, is that the ideological forefathers of Zionism underestimated the emotional and cultural legacy of centuries of European stigmatization of Jews and Judaism, as had the ideologists of Jewish enlightenment before them, who had expected the powerful light of human reason to banish the darkness of prejudice. *Maskilim*, liberal integrationists, Zionists, Bundists, communists – none realized how deeply embedded the stigmatization of Jews and Judaism was and is in Western culture – in its patterns of thought, sentiment, and expression. Just as the legislative and judicial achievements of the civil rights movement in the United States failed to banish contempt for and fear of African-Americans, so too consciousness of the Holocaust and the antisemitism that made it possible failed to destroy the legacy of centuries of Christian contempt. Lest I be misunderstood, let me be absolutely clear: I am not saying that non-Jews are hard-wired or genetically programmed to dislike Jews. I have no idea when and where and under what circumstances antisemitism will disappear in public and private life or even if it ever will. All I am claiming is that tropes and myths about Jews are more deeply embedded in Western culture than the intellectual heirs of the Enlightenment believed. Of course, there is less recourse to them today than there was before the war, but they still have life in them and can be mobilized at moments when Jews enter the public arena, as happens whenever the Israeli-Palestinian conflict becomes headline news.

What then causes Europeans to employ discredited antisemitic notions? Part of the answer, sadly, is their very consciousness of the enormity of the Holocaust and their responsibility for it. It is not coincidental that references to Nazism abound in recent European attacks on Jews and Israel. Rather, it is all too enlightening. Much of the impulse to denounce Israel and its supporters flows from a desire to turn the tables on Jews and displace feelings of Holo-caust-related guilt. For half a century, Jews and non-Jews alike have been telling Europeans – perpetrators, collaborators, and indifferent bystanders alike – that they bear responsibility for the murder of 6 million Jews – which, indeed, they (or at least their ancestors) do. The use of terms like 'war crimes,' 'crimes against humanity,' and 'genocide' and the explicit comparison of Israel to Nazi Ger-many represent an effort to displace feelings of guilt and responsibility. In the mental economy of those who use this kind of language, Europeans do not need to feel bad about what they did or failed to do during the war because, in the end, Jews/Israelis are no better than Nazis. Those who have been pointing their finger at us, they reason, are themselves no better. What right do they have to accuse us?! In this turning of the tables, the Jews are the new perpetrators, the Palestinians the new victims.[14] As my colleague Andrei Markovits has noted, there is a liberating dimension to this criticism of Jews. 'By constantly bringing up the truly shameful and disgusting analogy of the Israelis with the Nazis, Europeans absolve themselves from any remorse and shame ...' It is as if they are shouting, 'Free at last, free at last, we are finally free of this damn Holocaust at last.' The lid is off. The allegedly Jewish-imposed taboo is lifted. They can speak their minds once again.[15] As a member of the House of Lords with strong liberal credentials told Petronella Wyatt, columnist for the London

Evening Standard, in December 2001, 'The Jews have been asking for it and now, thank God, we can say what we think at last.'[16] Or, as the Spanish feminist Pilar Rahola told an interviewer in October 2002, Europe has 'a bad conscience.' 'It knows it is guilty' and has looked for 'expiation for its guilt' and found it in the Palestinian cause. 'The more the Jews are presented as being the evil party, the bad ones, the less difficult it is to carry the responsibility and the guilt.'[17]

A terrible irony lurks behind this psychological transaction. In blaming Jews for the suffering of Palestinians and casting the former as Nazis, West Europeans forget that were it not for their own intolerance there would have been little need to create a Jewish state in the first place. The impetus for Zionism was the failure of Jewish emancipation, the inability of Europeans in the nineteenth and early twentieth centuries to let go of old fears and hatreds and accept the presence of Jews in their midst. (In the Russian empire, emancipation was never even a serious political option.) Had European Jewry enjoyed legal equality and social acceptance, they would not have looked outside Europe for refuge and salvation. In other words, there is a double displacement of responsibility at work in the mental economy of West Europeans. Their unwillingness to accept Jews as fellow citizens and social equals between the French Revolution and the First World War created the foundation for the growth of Zionism in the first place. Then their active persecution of Jews during the Second World War – or their indifference to their fate – convinced Jews even more of the absolute necessity of creating a sovereign state in the Land of Israel. Having done their best in the nineteenth and twentieth centuries to make Jewish integration and acceptance difficult or even impossible, West Europeans now condemn them for settling in their ancient homeland. It is a classic instance of 'damned if you do, damned if you don't.'

In accounting for the prominence of the left (liberals and radicals alike) in the articulation of the new antisemitism, there are additional causes at work. First, in the last half-century, the left has regularly championed the cause of Third World, non-Western peoples. It has viewed them as victims of Western oppression (imperialism, colonialism, capitalism, globalization, racism, orientalism, etc.) and their use of violence as morally justified. At the same time, it has turned a blind eye to the tyranny, corruption, and mass murder that have flourished in so many postcolonial Third World states. The left enthusiastically mobilizes to denounce Israel, but not the gangster-like rule of Robert Mugabe in Zimbabwe or the slave trade carried on by Muslims in the Sudan. Most importantly, the left has romanticized postcolonial peoples and their struggles, making them the bearers of progressive values and representatives of moral authenticity, regardless of whether there is any factual basis for this. This is an old move on the part of European intellectuals, dating at least to the Enlightenment's use of Persian, Hindu, and Chinese sages to criticize old-regime European institutions and values. It is a species of orientalism – that is, of the Western world's discursive use of non-Western peoples for its own ends. That said, it should be no surprise that the West European left has adopted uncritically the Palestinian cause, which can be viewed as progressive simply because its opponent, Israel, is a Western state and a close ally of the arch-Satan, the United States. In the early twenty-first century, the Palestinians play the same role in the imagination of the European left that other progressive, freedom-loving peoples, including the Cubans, the Vietnamese, the Nicara-guans, and the Chinese, played earlier. Just as radical-minded college students once travelled to Castro's Cuba to help harvest sugar cane, their counterparts today rush to join Yassar Arafat in his compound in Ramallah.

Moreover, even if this analysis of *why* the West European left has embraced the Palestinians falls short of the mark, the fact remains that it has embraced them and made their struggle its own. Anti-Zionism has become an integral part of liberal and especially radical political rhetoric. To be a man or woman of the left is to think the worst of Israel from the very start. It comes with the territory. For the West European left, anti-Zionism has come to function like opposition to abortion for the American right and support for affirmative action for the American left. The inseparability of anti-Zionism from left political culture also explains why so many Jewish writers, artists, and academics in Europe rush to align themselves with left-wing criticism of Israel. By virtue of their Jewishness, their credentials as men and women of the left are open to suspicion. By loudly declaring their anti-Zionism, they confirm their bona fides as progressives. In this, they resemble those Jewish converts to Christianity in medieval and early modern Europe who became missionaries and polemicists for their new faith and thereby silenced their own doubts – and those of old Christians as well – about the depth and sincerity of their conversion.

Heightened anti-Americanism in the aftermath of the World Trade Center attack has also strengthened anti-Jewish sentiment in Western Europe. To explain the sharp rise in hostility to the United States would take us too far afield. Suffice it to say that both Jews and Israel have suffered for their identification with the United States, Israel's chief big-power supporter since the 1970s. For the right, both Jews and the United States represent unfettered, soulless modernity and the subversion of tradition. For the left, they represent unbridled capitalism, rampant individualism, consumerism, and materialism. If the United States is evil because it is the sole superpower (and allegedly building a global empire) and simultaneously the most vocal and visible friend of Israel, then by extension, Israel – industrial, open market, democratic, with the most robust economy in the Middle East – must be evil and its enemies virtuous. This explains, for example, why the antiglobalization movement has thrown its support to the Palestinians and why Jose Bové, the French sheep farmer with the walrus moustache, celebrated for wrecking McDonald's outlets and destroying genetically modified crops, travelled to the West Bank to denounce Israeli activity there.[18] This also explains why antiwar demonstrations in Europe's capitals in the months before the American invasion of Iraq became sites of crude Israel-bashing. In Paris, for example, protesters carried banners showing the Magen David intertwined with the swastika and proclaiming, 'Hitler, Bush, Sharon, in the name of God we kill.'[19] Significantly, the left was generally sympathetic to Israel between 1948 and 1967, when it was relatively weak, could be cast as the underdog, and received little American backing. Only when the Palestinians emerged as a nation and claimed the role of underdog and the Soviet Union became the chief sponsor of Egypt and Syria and the United States the chief backer of Israel did the left turn with a vengeance against Israel. More generally, it may be that Europeans on both the right and the left are sympathetic to Jews only when they are powerless and victimized. Powerful Jews who refuse to play the role of the weak underdog and seek to chart their own destiny may be too disturbing.

On balance, the new antisemitism is worrisome but not yet threatening. Like the old antisemitism, it draws strength and support from political causes that have little connection to the activities of real, flesh-and-blood Jews. And, like the old antisemitism, it incorporates and exploits powerful myths and images drawn from classical, pre-modern, Christian anti-Judaism. But the new antisemitism is not in any sense a replay of the old. At present, it does not threaten the prosperity and safety of most West European Jews. In France, perhaps an exception to this generalization, Muslim youth, drunk on the heady rhetoric of radical Islam, do threaten Jews. Initially, officials there were unwilling to acknowledge that antisemitism was again raising its ugly head and that Jews qua Jews were being targeted. As the situation worsened, they took a more activist stance. In general, West European governments now seem willing and able to contain the threat of anti-Jewish violence. Certainly, as individuals, Jews continue to prosper and play highly visible roles in political and cultural life, far more so than they did in the interwar years. But at the communal or collective level, Jewish interests – in particular, Jewish concern with the health and security of the Jewish state – are more vulnerable. This is very different from the threat posed by right-wing, ultra-nationalist antisemitism before the Second World War, whose goal was banishing Jews to the margins of society or, in the case of Nazism, destroying them altogether. In today's Europe, Jews have enemies on both the left and the right, and thus can no longer look to the left to defend their interests. Familiarity with the past would not have prepared one for this turn of events – few could have predicted it a decade ago – but familiarity with the past does allow one to see what is genuinely novel in this situation.

NOTES

1 Michel Gurfinkiel, 'France's Jewish Problem,' *Commentary* (July/August 2002); Craig S. Smith, 'French Jews Tell of a New and Threatening Wave of Anti-Semitism,' *New York Times*, 22 March 2003.

2 *Jewish Chronicle*, 1 February 2002.

3 Stephen Pollard, 'Now I Know That I Will Always Be an Outsider in Britain,' *Independent*, 1 May 2002.

4 Gabriel Schoenfeld, 'Israel and the Anti-Semites,' *Commentary* (June 2002).

5 Nonna Mayer, 'Is France Antisemitic?' *Sh'ma* (November 2002): 4.

6 *Forward*, 1 November 2002. These figures are slightly higher than those reported by the ADL. The ADL's figures were combined averages that gave equal weight to each of the five states despite great differences in their populations. The *Forward* staff recalculated the data constructing a sample that was weighted for the relative size of the population of each country.

7 Murray Gordon, 'The New Anti-Semitism in Western Europe.' Available online: http://www.ajc.org/InTheMedia/Publications.

8 Shulamit Volkov, 'Antisemitism as a Cultural Code: Reflections on the History and Historiography of Antisemitism in Imperial Germany,' *Leo Baeck Institute Year Book* 23 (1978): 25–46.

9 Quoted in Gurfinkiel, 'France's Jewish Problem.' In fall 2002, a group of teachers published a book in which they claimed that it had become impossible to teach the Holocaust in some classrooms because of the hostility of Muslim students to the subject. *Les territoires perdus de la République: Antisémitisme, racisme et sexisme en milieu scolaire* (Paris: Mille et une nuits, 2002).

10 Marc Perelman, 'French Minister Unveils Plan to Fight Antisemitism,' *Forward*, 7 March 2003; and Perelman, 'A Tough-talking French Minister Raps Arabs, Left on Antisemitism,' *Forward*, 21 March 2003.

11 Or, in the words of Roger Cukierman, president of France's largest Jewish communal organization (CRIF), when 'a country the size of two or three French *départements*' becomes 'the crux of the planet's injustices.' Michel Zlotowski, '"Frightening" Anti-Israel Alliance of Left and Right,' *Jewish Chronicle*, 31 January 2003.

12 Thomas L. Friedman, 'A Middle Eastern Revolution,' *International Herald Tribune*, 27 February 2003.

13 Rather than pursue the question analytically, Sigmund Freud despairingly concluded, 'With regard to anti-semitism I don't really want to search for explanations: I feel a strong inclination to surrender to my affects in this matter and find myself confirmed in my wholly non-scientific belief that mankind on the average and taken by and large are a wretched lot.' Ernest L. Freud, ed., *The Letters of Sigmund Freud and Arnold Zweig*, trans. Elaine and William Robson-Scott (New York: Harcourt, Brace and World, 1970), 3.

14 On this theme, see Alvin H. Rosenfeld, 'The Growing Unease among Germany's Jews.' Available online: http://www.ajc.org/InTheMedia/Publications.

15 Andrei S. Markovits, 'Europe's Unified Voice and Passion,' *Sh'ma* (November 2002): 1.

16 Quoted in Norman Gelb, 'Out of the Closet: The New Face of British Antisemitism,' *The New Leader* (March/April 2002).

17 Pilar Rahola, interview with Marc Tobias; trans. David A. Harris, *Wexner Heritage Foundation, World Jewry Update*, 2 December 2002. Available online: http://www.wexnerheritage.org.

18 Phil Reeves, 'Jose Bové Takes His Magic Potion to the West Bank,' *Independent*, 21 June 2001.

19 Elaine Sciolino, 'French Rallies against War Shift Focus to Israel,' *New York Times*, 30 March 2003.

Chapter 6

Antisemitism and Anti-Zionism: A Historical Approach

DEREK J. PENSLAR

Attitudes towards Jews and Judaism in the contemporary Middle East are often informed by antisemitism. Accusations of international Jewish political and financial conspiracies, comparisons between Jews and Nazis, Holocaust denial, and claims that Israelis have introduced toxic chemicals and lethal viruses into the Occupied Territories are all redolent of the Jew-hatred of earlier eras. But alongside this irrational discourse on Jewish malevolent power is a more rational critique of Zionism and Israel as they really are, as political opponents of the Arab world, as claimants to territories that Palestinians believe are rightfully theirs. Derek Penslar's essay explores questions of continuity and rupture between antisemitism and Arab anti-Zionism through an unusual route. He offers a close reading of late-nineteenth- through mid-twentieth-century European antisemites' views of Zionism – views that were utterly irrational and divorced from reality – and compares these views with Arab perspectives on Zionism from the late 1800s to our own day.

* * *

In his classic Zionist manifesto *The Jewish State* (1896), Theodor Herzl claimed that the 'Jewish Question' was a matter 'to be managed through counsel with the civilized nations of the globe.'[1] Herzl believed that, although antisemitism in Europe was pervasive, irrational, and ineradicable, Zionism offered a rational response to the problem, and so the same 'civilized nations' in which antisemitism flourished would also gladly support and help organize the mass movement of Jews to Palestine.

In 1978, some eighty years after the publication of *The Jewish State*, Yehoshafat Harkabi, an Israeli scholar of the modern Arab world and Israeli security policy, wrote an intriguing analysis of antisemitism in the contemporary Arab world.

Harkabi argued that Arab antisemitism was the product of a specific political conflict – the century-long struggle with the Zionist movement, the *Yishuv*, and State of Israel – as opposed to the Islamic religious tradition as such or a fundamental inability of Islamic lands to tolerate Jews in their midst.[2] In an earlier work, Harkabi had documented at considerable length the extent of Judeophobic fantasy in the Arab world, and he made no effort now to deny or belittle the findings from his previous research.[3] But Harkabi came to question the value of cataloguing hostile statements about Israel or Jews without taking into account the historical circumstances in which they emerged or noting, as one could see during the era of the Camp David peace accords, that the same government directives that stoked antisemitic rhetoric could also staunch it, and that Arab attitudes towards Israel were shaped as much by specific Israeli policies and actions as by inherited, pervasive antisemitic stereotypes.

Whereas for Herzl antisemitism was an irrational sentiment that could be controlled through rational state action, for Harkabi, Arab anti-Zionism began as a rational response to a genuine threat but then mutated into irrational behaviour by governing elites. Or, to employ a medical metaphor – quite appropriate, since all forms of antisemitism are pathological – European antisemitism may be compared to a psychosomatic illness, whereas its Arab counterpart more closely resembles a toxic allergic reaction. The former originates in fantasy yet cripples the entire body politic; the latter is a debilitating, even fatal, response to a genuine substance.

Both of these two approaches – one towards antisemitism in *fin de siècle* Europe, the other towards Arab antipathy towards Jews and Israel – understand antisemitism to be a response to apparently inexplicable upheavals and an expression of virulent *ressentiment*. Examining the two together allows us to draw a crucial distinction between the realms of systemic intolerance aggravated by socio-economic crisis, and political strife driven by discrete events and policies. Comparing European and Arab antisemitism can illuminate the historic commonalities and distinctions between antisemitism and anti-Zionism and clarify the nature of antisemitism in our own day.

Whereas most studies of the relationship between antisemitism and anti-Zionism focus on contemporary developments, I intend to highlight the period from the 1870s to the early 1930s, when, in parallel fashion, antisemitism became a mobilizing, all-embracing ideology in Europe, while the Arab world witnessed an eruption of anticolonial and nationalist sentiment, often directed against the Zionist project. I am particularly interested in *fin de siècle* European antisemites' attitudes towards Zionism, which, I will show, were fundamentally different from anti-Zionist rhetoric emanating from the Middle East at that time. There is value in grasping underlying assumptions and visceral feelings about Zionism when they were first expressed, before they were affected by contingencies and rapidly changing events on the ground. In the early 1900s, and particularly after the proclamation of the Balfour Declaration in 1917 and the rapid growth of the Jewish National Home thereafter, Zionism was a sufficiently powerful presence on the international scene and within Palestine itself to command attention without being so influential that it had to be accorded de facto acceptance or utterly demonized.

* * *

Classic, nineteenth-century antisemitism identified the Jew with modern capitalism and the rapid transformation of society and culture that came in its wake. Ancient and medieval tropes of Jewish avarice, murderous hatred of Gentiles, and black-magical practices mutated into the modern stereotype of an international Jewish conspiracy. Tellingly, the myth of a global Jewish financial cabal flourished among early socialist thinkers in France and Germany during the 1840s, a decade of economic turmoil due in part to the impact of industrialization on the peasants and artisans who constituted the bulk of the population. The metonymic association between Jew and capitalism, and by extension with modernity as such, was a driving force behind late-nineteenth-century political antisemitism, described appositely by the German socialist leader August Bebel as 'the socialism of the stupid man.'

Intriguingly, the discourse on Jewish restoration to Palestine, a discourse that intensified with the writings of the former socialist Moses Hess in the 1860s and, of course, with the establishment of the Zionist movement in the 1880s, attracted little sustained attention from antisemitic ideologues. To be sure, one can find scattered statements in writings on the 'Jewish Question,' dating back to the Enlightenment, about shipping Jews out of Europe and back to Palestine. Scholars have painstakingly accumulated such statements by the likes of Johann Gottfried von Herder, Johann Gottlieb Fichte, Pierre-Joseph Proudhon, Heinrich von Treitschke, and Adolph Stöcker, among others, but they have failed to note that these utterances were merely barbed quips or enraged outbursts and rarely led to a sustained engagement with Zionism, even after Theodor Herzl brought it on to the stage of public opinion.

One apparent exception was the Hungarian antisemitic activist Gyözö Istóczy, who is the subject of a recent biography by Andrew Handler provocatively titled *An Early Blueprint for Zionism*. Handler draws the title from a speech of 1878 on 'The Restoration of the Jewish State in Palestine' delivered by Istóczy from the floor of the Hungarian Diet, of which he was an elected member.

Reflecting an anti-Russian and pro-Turkish sentiment as much as an antisemitic world view, Istóczy claimed that such a state would revive 'the enfeebled and backward East' by introducing Jewish wealth and energy, 'a vigorous, powerful and new element and an influential ingredient of civilization.'[4] Istóczy offered few specifics as to how this plan would be implemented, and subsequent to the speech Istóczy soon let the matter drop, as it encountered strong disapproval from his fellow parliamentarians. Thus this 'early blueprint' for Zionism was, in fact, quite sketchy and faded quickly.[5]

By and large, antisemitic ideologues of the *fin de siècle* paid Zionism little heed, and when they did think about it, dismissed it as a trick, perpetrated by the agents of the international Jewish conspiracy. In the French journalist Edouard Drumont, perhaps the most successful antisemitic scribbler of the period, we have the interesting case of an antisemite whose interest in Zionism waxed and waned, fading away altogether when Drumont decided that Zionism did not stand a chance against its rivals, assimilationist and plutocratic Jews, who also happened to be, in Drumont's view, the greatest threats to the world as a whole.

Drumont's daily newspaper, *La Libre Parole*, greeted the first Zionist Congress of 1897 with great fanfare. Apparently confirming Herzl's views that antisemites and Zionists would find a meeting of minds and form a productive collaboration, the newspaper wrote, in its customary sneering tone, 'Not only does [*La Libre Parole*] offer, freely and enthusiastically, publicity for the [Zionist] colonists , but if it were ever – an inconceivable thing – a question of money that caused the Jews to hesitate, it takes upon itself the commitment to take up a subscription whose immense success is not in doubt.'[6] Yet right from the start Drumont saw a snake in the Zionist garden, Jewish '*haute-banque*,' that cabal of powerful Jewish financiers whose economic interests depended on the mainte-nance of a vast global Jewish network and would thus be harmed by the mass movement of Jews to Palestine.[7]

By 1913 Drumont had given up on Zionism. On the eve of the Eleventh Zionist Congress, Drumont warned darkly that 'this conference will probably be the last, and this racket will have sounded Zionism's death-knell.'[8] Drumont noted darkly that the 'great Jews' Herzl and Max Nordau, Herzl's lieutenant, had been vanquished by the combined forces of assimilationists and Jewish high finance. Drumont accused the former of shifting the Zionist Organization's focus away from international diplomacy aimed at obtaining a Jewish home-land secured by public law and enmeshing the movement in political and cultural activity in the diaspora. Even worse, according to Drumont, was the work of 'the great Jews, the aristocrats of banking,' who had always been hostile to Zionism, and who had now created Territorialism, a movement to set up Jewish enclaves throughout the world, thereby allowing the Jewish financiers to further extend their tentacles of political and economic control.

It matters little that Drumont was wrong on both points – both increased diaspora activism and Territorialism developed from within the heart of the Zionist movement. Rather, the key here is that Drumont placed the contest between Zionism and its enemies within sturdy and venerable antisemitic frameworks of conspiracy led by Jewish plutocrats and cultural domination by assimilated Jewish intellectuals. Drumont's views on Zionism were not influenced by, nor did they influence, his general antisemitic world view. Drumont was willing to endorse Zionism if it appeared to confirm his pre-existing views that Jewish nationhood was ineradicable, but at the blink of an eye he was quite willing to disown it, especially since, on the eve of and during the First World War, Zionist goals increasingly appeared to conflict with French imperial interests and the sensibilities of Roman Catholics in the Middle East.[9]

In France, Zionism, although occasionally applauded or derided, appears to have been peripheral to the antisemitic imagination. None of the voluminous adulatory literature written in France about Drumont in the decades following his death – literature that includes generous extracts from his work – makes so much as a mention of Zionism. Such books do, however, faithfully reproduce Drumont's own *idées fixes* about Jewish responsibility for the corruption, social upheaval, and financial scandals that were making life hell for the little man.[10]

In Germany, by contrast, from the 1870s onward, antisemites were wont to judge Zionism more harshly, as a manifestation of ongoing global Jewish chicanery. Wilhelm Marr, who is credited with coining the term 'antisemitism' in the late 1870s, wrote here and there throughout the 1880s about shipping all of Europe's Jews to Palestine, where they could put their boundless energy and resources to work in creating a model polity, a *Musterstaat*. Yet this relatively sanguine attitude did not survive the passage of time, as Marr's antisemitic world view grew ever darker and more bitter. Marr wrote at the time of the First Zionist Congress of 1897 that 'the entire matter is a foul Jewish swindle, in order to divert the attention of the European peoples from the Jewish problem.'[11] Marr did not elaborate on his opposition to Zionism, for, as with Drumont and the other antisemites we have analysed thus far, Zionism was far from central to Marr's concerns.

The logical connection between conspiratorial antisemitism and an adamant rejection of Zionism may be found in the work of Marr's contemporary, Eugen Dühring, author of what was perhaps the most relentlessly brutal antisemitic tract of the late nineteenth century, *The Jewish Question as a Question of Racial Noxiousness for the Existence, Morals and Culture of Nations* (1881). This book, which went through six editions up to 1930, offers an opportunity to observe how an acutely intelligent but deranged individual responded to Zionism as the movement gained prominence from the 1880s through the end of the First World War. We see that it was precisely the depth of Dühring's antisemitism that prevented him from taking Zionism seriously and considering it outside of the pre-packaged framework of a Jewish financial and cultural stranglehold over all of Europe. In the 1892 edition, Dühring devotes more than seventy pages to elaborately detailed 'solutions' to the 'Jewish Problem' – solutions that included reducing the numbers of Jews in, or barring them altogether from, the civil service, professions, journalism, and teaching, and laying punitive taxes on Jewish-owned banks and other enterprises. In short, Dühring advocates the de-emancipation of European Jewry. Claiming that the Jews are racially incorrigible and disposed to parasitism and nomadism, Dühring dismisses Zionism in a couple of paragraphs, claiming that Jews would always prefer living under the most oppressive conditions among Gentiles than among their own kind, whom they would find it difficult to exploit.[12]

As Dühring aged, his language grew ever more bilious and threatening. In the posthumously published 1930 edition of the work, Dühring claimed that throughout history no political force had been able to contain the Jewish menace. The Roman conquest of Palestine merely spread the Jewish disease into the diaspora, expulsion decrees in medieval Europe were ineffective, and ghettoization served only to strengthen Jewish solidarity. Today, a Jewish state would only accentuate Jewish power; the Jewish snake that encircles the globe would now have a head:

> This would entail pushing history back, thereby making necessary something like a second Roman clearing action. It would mean going back to the beginning, where the matter would be brought to an end in an entirely different and far more comprehensive sense. [*Es hiesse zum Anfang zurückzukehren, wo in einem ganz andern und weit durchgreifenderen Sinne ein Ende zu machen ist.*][13]

A chilling, and prescient, threat indeed, yet one made in passing, via a few sentences, after which Dühring returns to his favourite themes of Jewish control over most aspects of politics, economics, and culture in the Western world.

Like any antisemitic ideologue, Dühring had to simultaneously fabricate falsehood and deny reality. Not only does he demonize Zionist international diplomatic and fund-raising activity, he also ignores the growth of the Jewish National Home, which was rooted in notions of Jewish bodily and cultural renewal. Like utraviolet light, invisible to the naked eye, many aspects of the

Zionist project simply could not be perceived within the optical field of antisemitism. For antisemites, Zionism was nothing but smoke and mirrors, and the only appropriate response was to conjure it away.

An association between Zionism and Jewish criminality became central to Nazi ideology, pioneered by Alfred Rosenberg, who claimed in 1922 that Zionism was an anti-German movement that drew support from reactionary capitalists (the Rothschilds) and communists ('Jewish' Bolsheviks) alike. Drawing on Rosenberg and Dühring, Adolf Hitler, writing in *Mein Kampf*, would claim that Jews have no intention or ability to construct a legitimate state in Palestine, but rather wish to make it into a clearing house for their international economic swindling operations: '[E]ndowed with sovereign rights and removed from the intervention of other states,' a Jewish state would become 'a haven for convicted scoundrels and a university for budding crooks.'[14] (Thus the intellectual pedigree of notorious contemporary Holocaust denier Ernst Zundel's characterization of Israel as 'a gangster enclave in the Middle East.')[15]

Even in Nazi ideology, however, Zionism was little more than an addendum to a well-worn diatribe against international Jewish political machinations and inveterate malevolence. The presence of the Zionist movement did not substantively add to or detract from pre-existing modes of antisemitic sensibility. The conceptual irrelevance of Zionism behind modern European antisemitism is demonstrated all the more clearly by the most significant text in the history of twentieth-century antisemitism, *The Protocols of the Elders of Zion*.

The precise authorship of the *Protocols* remains obscure, but scholars concur that the work was written by agents of the Russian secret police in Paris at the turn of the last century. The *Protocols* was the most notorious expression of Jewish conspiracy theory, which originated among opponents of the Enlightenment and French Revolution. Specifically, the *Protocols* was inspired by Hermann Goedsche's novel *Biarritz* (1868), a section of which depicts the assembly of a Jewish cabal at a Prague cemetery. Much of the *Protocols'* text, however, was plagiarized from a second, wholly innocuous work, Maurice Joly's *A Dialogue in Hell* (1864), which employed a fictional dialogue between the philosophers Machiavelli and Montesquieu in order to satirize the authoritarian rule of the French emperor Napoleon III. The authors of the *Protocols* lifted many of Machiavelli's speeches verbatim and put them into the mouths of Jewish conspirators. Yet the authors of the *Protocols* transmuted Joly's text while plagiarizing it, in that Joly presented Machiavelli as a cynical realist, whereas the *Protocols* depicts the Jews as the embodiment of preternatural, all consuming evil.[16]

Antisemitism in *fin de siècle* West and Central Europe could be a form of lower-middle-class protest: in Germany and Austria, it took the form of

'Christian socialism' and nourished the populist demagoguery of Vienna's mayor Karl Lueger. In Russia, on the other hand, antisemitism was often reactionary, a rejection of modernity in any form and a paean to rigid hierarchical rule by a hereditary nobility. These sentiments pervade the *Protocols*, which was written primarily in order to sabotage Russia's halting moves towards economic modernization by associating liberalization with Jewish conspiracy. The link between Russia, reaction, and the *Protocols* was strengthened by its publication in St Petersburg in 1903. The *Protocols* was disseminated throughout Russia by members of the ultra-rightist Black Hundreds, and Tsar Nicholas and Tsarina Alexandra commanded that Orthodox priests declaim the *Protocols* in the churches of Moscow.

In its early editions, a variety of origins were attributed to the *Protocols*, and only after the First World War do we see a popularization and routinization of the claim that it transcribes deliberations from the First Zionist Congress. The references to Herzl and the Congress come at the very beginning of the texts, and nothing in the text of the *Protocols* itself touches upon Zionism, although the *Protocols* was forged at the time of the beginnings of political Zionism in the late 1890s. Significantly, in editions of the *Protocols* issued before 1917, the international Jewish body referred to most often as generating the text is the French-Jewish global philanthropic organization the Alliance Israelite Universelle. (A spectacular, but anomalous exception was the work of the Russian adventuress L. Fry, who claimed that the Zionist intellectual Ahad Ha-Am penned the *Protocols*.)[17] Just as the internationalist dimension of the Alliance's name and activities stoked the antisemitic imagination of the *fin de siècle*, so could the increased visibility of the Zionist movement in the wake of the Balfour Declaration and establishment of the British Mandate over Palestine encourage antisemites to interpret the Basel Congress as, citing Norman Cohn, 'a giant stride towards Jewish world-domination.'[18] But the actual Zionist program, enunciated at Basel in 1897 and legitimized in part by the British in 1917 and 1920, of creating a Jewish National Home in Palestine is overlooked in the interwar editions of the *Protocols*. Even the notorious paraphrase of the *Protocols* serialized in Henry Ford's *Dearborn Independent* in 1920, which claims that the Sixth Zionist Congress predicted the outbreak of the First World War and that the Zionist movement represents the tip of an iceberg of international Jewish power, only engages issues relating to Jewish political activity in interwar Europe, specifically the minority rights treaties, which allegedly singled Jews out for favourable treatment.[19]

To sum up, Zionism did not exist as a discrete phenomenon in the minds of European antisemites during the half-century prior to the Holocaust. It was merely a placeholder for a host of conspiratorial fantasies that were rooted deep in the nineteenth century and in a search for an identifiable agent responsible for the bewildering social and political transformations sweeping Europe like a storm. Jews were, of course, only occasional representatives, rather than creators or agents, of these processes, as the antisemite's Jew was little more than a reflection and reification of European society itself. Granted, although European antisemitism was riddled with contradictions and highly irrational, it was not wholly illogical. It attributed to the Jew only selected attributes of the human psyche, such as arrogance, cupidity, and a thirst for power. The antisemite's Jew was not stupid, brutish, or enslaved to passion. Bridging the clashing stereotypes of the Jewish capitalist and communist was an underlying and unifying reality: the Jews' historic prominence in the economy's distributive sector and as agents of economic change. Even so, the visibility of Jews in commerce and the medical and legal professions was a symptom, not a cause, of a capitalist economic order with a meritocratic impetus and a permeable elite. The 'Jewish Question' in modern Europe did not amount to anything more than a deceptively tangible avatar of the 'social question.' Zionism as an ideology and political movement did not impinge upon the lives of Europeans as did other forces associated with Jews, such as capitalism, Bolshevism, or cultural modernism.

* * *

The function of Zionism in modern Arab antisemitism is radically different from its European counterpart. Whereas European antisemites regarded Zionism as a manifestation of Judaism, in the Middle East Jews and Judaism have, for the past century or more, been defined in terms of Zionism. In making this claim I do not mean to travel along the lines of post-1948 Arab propagandists who have presented the history of the Jews in the lands of Islam as uniformly stable and prosperous, blessed by Islam's enlightened and tolerant attitude towards its protected minorities, an attitude overturned solely by the injustices and cruelties against Arabs perpetrated by the state of Israel.[20] Obviously, the fate of Jews in *dar al-Islam* has often been an unhappy one, moulded in part by the Judeophobic motifs that are embedded in Islam's foundational texts. In addition to the Koran's many polemical comments about Jews and its accounts of Jewish treachery against Muhammad, a traditional biography of Muhammed attributes his death to poisoning by a Jewish woman, and an equally venerable historical text claims that Shi'ism, which sundered Islamic unity, was instigated by a Yemenite Jew.[21] Such texts, however, mean little when not considered in the context of medieval Jewish life in the lands of Islam, where despite constant discrimination the Jews lived in greater security, and were far less often the subject of chimeric fantasy, than in Europe, where persecutions and expulsions of Jews often followed accusations of ritual murder, desecration of the sacred host, and consorting with the Devil. As Mark Cohen has argued convincingly in his comparative history of Jewish life in medieval Christendom and *dar al-Islam*, in the latter, acts of expulsion and forced conversion were highly exceptional.[22] Today, many critics of Muslim antisemitism place great stock in Moses Maimonides' celebrated *Letter to the Jews of Yemen* (1172), in which the renowned scholar claimed that the lot of Jews has been far worse under Muslim than Christian rule. Yet this was a *cri de coeur* issued in a time of extreme, and atypical, persecution.

In the nineteenth century, notions of a Jewish international political and financial conspiracy were exported to the Middle East, largely via French and francophone Christian clerics. Intriguingly, however, during the late Ottoman era, Arab opposition to Zionism was not necessarily antisemitic. Palestinian Arabs expressed rational fears of displacement from a land in which they had long been resident, and Ottoman officials worried about the creation in the empire of a new minority problem akin to that presented by the Armenians.[23] Similarly, the *fin de siècle* Muslim reformer Rashid Rida believed Jews to comprise a unified, wealthy, and powerful collective, but his concern was the reality presented by the immigration of tens of thousands of Jews into Palestine, not, as in the case of European antisemitism, broad social transformations in which Jews played no significant causal role.

The secular Arab nationalist Najib Azuri, writing in 1905 in his classic work *Le Réveil de la nation arabe*, described Jews as a people engaged in a concerted drive to establish a state in what they perceived to be their homeland. 'On the final outcome of this struggle,' Azuri noted darkly (and, one hopes, not presciently), 'between these two peoples, representing two opposing principles, will depend the destiny of the entire world.'[24] Azuri's casual reference to Jews as a people points out an interesting distinction between early-twentieth-century Arab anti-Zionism, on the one hand, and both European antisemitism and later forms of Arab anti-Zionism, on the other. It was a staple of European antisemitism that Judaism comprised both a nation and a religion.

Unlike European antisemitism, which imagined Jews to constitute an unassimilable and noxious nation, defying the quid pro quo of assimilation for emancipation, in the decades after Azuri, Arab propaganda had to develop an opposite argument that the Jews did not constitute even a retrograde nation, for to admit as much might open the way to accepting the legitimacy of the principles of Zionism.

In the twentieth-century Arab world, the interlacing of antisemitic motifs with opposition to Zionism occurred in a direct response to increased Jewish immigration to Palestine. It is no coincidence that the *Protocols of the Elders of Zion* first appeared in Arabic in 1925, during the fourth, and largest yet, wave of Zionist immigration to Palestine. (The translation, from the French, was the work of a Catholic priest, Antoine Yamin, in Egypt.) The following year, an article in a periodical of the Jerusalem Latin Patriarchate announced the presence of the Arabic translation of the *Protocols* and urged the faithful to read it in order to understand what the Zionists had in store for Palestine. During the disturbances of the years 1928–9, Haj Amin al-Huayni, the mufti of Jerusalem, publicized portions of the *Protocols* in connection with alleged Jewish plots to conquer the Temple Mount. Thus, although the translation was done by a Christian cleric, infused with European antisemitic sensibilities, the text was immediately introduced into the context of the new and unique political conflict between Arabs and Jews for control over Palestine.[25]

To be sure, during the interwar period, Arab antisemitism was nourished by sources outside of Palestine. The rapid social mobility and prominence of Jews in Middle Eastern lands under colonial rule and the economic and administrative links between Jews and colonial regimes instilled a powerful antisemitic element into Arab nationalist movements, for which Jews served as metonymic representations of the West. Middle Eastern antisemitism was strengthened further by the increasing popularity of socialism and communism among Arab intellectuals. Jews were defined by the Arab left as in league with their fascist persecutors, while royalists and fascist sympathizers leapt to wild conclusions from the disproportionate involvement of Jews in the communist parties in Egypt and Iraq. The important common element behind these contradictory expressions of Arab antisemitism during the interwar period was the adoption of common European views of the Jew as universal solvent, the destroyer of social order and bringer of chaos, housed in both the left and right ends of the political and economic spectrum. Arab antisemitism even adopted European notions of preternatural Jewish sexual powers. The secular and socialist-inspired youth so visible among the Zionist immigrants prompted Arab accusations that Jews were sexually promiscuous as well as carriers of Bolshevism – indeed, the Arab word for 'communist' was *ibahi*, 'permissive.'[26]

Nonetheless, up to 1948 Arab antisemitism did not routinely function, as it did in Europe, as a totally unbounded discourse, attributing every ill of modern humanity to Jewish influence. And within Palestine itself, antisemitism grew directly out of conflict with the Zionist movement and its gradual yet purposeful settlement of the country. The dominant tone was set as early as 1920, when in a play entitled *The Ruin of Palestine*, performed in Nablus, the comely daughter of a Jewish tavern keeper seduces two wealthy Arabs, coaxes out of them their money and even the deeds to their properties, leaving the Arabs with no resource other than suicide, before which they wail 'the country is ruined, the Jews have robbed us of our land and honour!'[27]

Our focus thus far on the period before 1948 sharpens our perception of the novel qualities of Arab antisemitic discourse generated since the creation of the State of Israel. As opposed to traditional Muslim Judeophobia, post-1948 Arab antisemitism featured a transition from a view of the Jew as weak and degraded to a belief in Jewish global power. Traditional Islam scorned the Jew; post-1948 Arab antisemitism has blended contempt with fear. The fear stems from the apparent inability of Arabs to stop what has seemed to them to be a well-coordinated Jewish takeover of Palestine, a land whose sanctity and significance has grown in the face of what appears to be a repetition of the Crusades, a European assault against the heartland of the Islamic world. Humiliating though it was to be subjugated by Christian Europe during the era of colonialism, it has been all the more galling to witness Palestine falling under the rule of Jews.

Indeed, the trope of assaulted Arab dignity is perhaps the most common theme in contemporary Arab antisemitism. Western pundits are wont to attribute this discourse to an atavistic shame-culture, in which codes of personal honour, particularly male honour, bind a rigid socioreligious hierarchy that privileges status over achievement and resists the formation of a liberal, inclusive, egalitarian and democratic Western-style civil society. It is not my brief to determine if such views are accurate or are the product of facile orientalist fantasies. What is clear, however, is that the discourse on dignity in the Middle East stems primarily from a sense of overwhelming helplessness rather than merely wounded pride. However much the Arab powers may have bickered over the fate of Palestine during the 1940s, the loss of Palestine to a Jewish state was seen as the defining catastrophic event of the era, or, as Constantine Zurayq described it in 1956, *al-Naqba*, a term that gained universal currency in decades to come:

> The defeat of the Arabs in Palestine is no simple setback or light, passing evil. It is a disaster in every sense of the word and one of the harshest trials and tribulations with which the Arabs have been afflicted throughout their long history – a history marked by numerous trials and tribulations.[28]

Regardless of how one apportions responsibility for *al-Naqba*, the conquest of the West Bank and Gaza in 1967, the ensuing occupation of those territories, and the steady settlement of Jews therein, all of these phenomena are historical realities, as is Israel's close relationship – particularly since 1967 – with the United States, which is widely seen in the Middle East as the last remaining great colonial power. There is an immeasurable gap between this scenario and that of modern Europe, where Jews as a collective wielded no power, conquered no land, expelled no family from its home.

There are strains of post-1948 Arab antisemitism that absorbed the Manichean qualities of Nazism, elevating the Jew into a global, even cosmic, evil, who must be annihilated, not only within Palestine but wherever he may be found. Such viewpoints are espoused vigorously by Muslim fundamentalists in many lands. They trace their intellectual pedigree to Sayyid Qutb, the intellectual father of the Muslim Brotherhood, who, while in Egyptian prisons during the 1950s, embroidered a European-style ontological antisemitism into his massive commentary on the Koran. Qutb's antisemitism was ontological, perceiving Jews as incorrigibly evil and associated with all the world's ills, including capitalism, communism, atheism, materialism, and modernism.[29] During the 1960s, Qutb, like fundamentalist leaders elsewhere in the Middle East, devoted most of his effort to toppling secular Arab leaders. Developments over a period of fifteen years – the 1967 war, the Sadat peace initiative, the Iranian Revolution, and Israel's invasion of Lebanon – transformed Muslim fundamentalism, causing anti-Zionism to, according to Emmanuel Sivan, 'take pride of place, presented as the modern-day incarnation of the authentically Islamic hostility to the Jews.'[30]

Nonetheless, the older, Palestinocentric streak in Arab antisemitism lives on in our own day, as in the recently aired Egyptian television serial *Horseman without a Horse*, which was based in part on the *Protocols of the Elders of Zion*, but in which the Jewish conspiracy to control the world is replaced by a specific plot to take control of Palestine. Moreover, it is significant that the *Protocols* comes in and out of fashion in Egypt; it was popular under Nasser, but fell out of circulation in the wake of Camp David, only to return after the failure of the Oslo peace accords. Arab antisemitism in any form is repugnant, but those forms that wax and wane in response to developments in Arab-Israeli relations are qualitatively different from the Manicheanism of extremist Muslim fundamentalists, who, no less than the Nazis, imagine Jews as literally the handmaids of Satan and call for their eradication from the face of the globe. It is essential to draw a clear distinction between these two different forms of antisemitism, one of which may be malleable, subject to change in a dynamic and constructive political environment, while the other kind is incurable and must be confronted with unequivocal condemnation, isolation, and, when necessary, forceful suppression.

I would like to conclude by linking the comparative framework constructed in this essay with another sort of comparison, one frequently invoked by those who see European and Arab antisemitism as of a piece and who associate anti-Zionism with antisemitism *tout court*. I am referring to the notion that Jews in modern times, ranging from nineteenth-century Europe to Israel today, have featured an exaggerated, perhaps unique, capacity for self-criticism, and that this practice has led Jews to internalize antisemitic assaults against them and to labour in vain to ingratiate themselves with their persecutors. There is the frequently cited example of nineteenth-century German Jews, who responded to antisemitic accusations of Jewish vulgarity and parasitism by encouraging circumspect public behaviour, the utmost probity in business affairs, and the promotion of reputable, honourable occupations in crafts among poor Jewish youth. Of course, nothing German Jews did could possibly mitigate antisemitism, let alone assuage the genocidal fury of the Nazis. Similarly, argue many staunch supporters of Israel today, leftist Israelis and their counterparts in the Jewish diaspora are urging that Israel make massive, and ultimately self-destructive, territorial and political sacrifices in an illusory pursuit of peace. According to this pessimistic world view, for most Arabs peace can only come in the wake of Israel's destruction, either spectacularly, by force, or gradually, through its transformation into a binational state, whose Jewish component would over time be overwhelmed by a rapidly growing Arab population, and whose Jewish character would accordingly fade away.

I respond to this objection by noting that Israel, unlike the Jewish global conspiracy of the European antisemitic imagination, does exist. Precisely be-cause Arab antisemitism's fantasies are far more thoroughly grounded in reality than those of their European predecessors, a necessary, although admittedly not sufficient, precondition for deconstructing those fantasies will be a radical transformation of Israel's borders and policies towards Arabs both within and outside of the state. As Yehoshafat Harkabi wrote in the wake of the Camp David summit, 'It is not the change of images ... which will lead to peace, but peace which will lead to the change of images.'[31] Unlike the decline of antisemitism in post-1945 Europe, which was not the work of Jews but rather the result of the crimes and guilt of European society as a whole, in the Middle East Jews are obliged to make fateful political decisions in the hopes that such decisions will stimulate equally constructive action on the part of Israel's neighbours and the Palestinians under its control, that these multilateral ac-tions will in fact lead to peace, and that peace will lead to a change of Arab images of Jews. This time around, antisemitism grows out of a political conflict in which Jews are empowered actors, not figments of the imagination. For this reason, although the chances for accommodation between Israel and the Arab world may appear slim, conditions are vastly more favourable than in pre-

Second World War Europe, not simply because the Jewish state possesses military power, but also because it has the capacity to take actions that may weaken the raison d'être of Arab antisemitism.

NOTES

1 Theodor Herzl, *Der Judenstaat*, 8th ed. (Berlin: Jüdisches Verlag, 1920), 9–10.

2 Yehoshafat Harkabi, 'On Arab Antisemitism Once More,' in Shmuel Almog, ed., *Antisemitism through the Ages* (Oxford: Pergamon, 1988), 227–40. The Hebrew edition, based on a 1978 conference, was published in 1980.

3 The book *Arab Attitudes to Israel*, published in English in 1971, first appeared in Hebrew in 1967.

4 Andrew Handler, *An Early Blueprint for Zionism: Győző Istóczy's Political Antisemitism* (Boulder: East European Monographs, Columbia University Press, 1989), 42–51.

5 Ibid., 152.

6 'Un Congrès Israélite,' *La Libre Parole*, 17 August 1897.

7 Le Sionisme et la haute banque,' *La Libre Parole*, 4 September 1897.

8 'L'Agonie du sionisme,' *La Libre Parole*, 11 September 1913.

9 'Le Congrès sioniste: Nouvelle orientation,' *La Libre Parole*, 31 August 1913; Frederick Busi, 'Anti-Semites on Zionism,' *Midstream* (February 1979): 18–27.

10 E.g., Georges Bernanos, *La Grande Peur des bien-pensants, Edouard Drumont* (Paris: B. Grasset, 1931); Henry Coston, *Signé Drumont* (Paris: H. Coston, 1997).

11 Moshe Zimmermann, *Wilhelm Marr: The Patriarch of Antisemitism* (New York: Oxford University Press, 1986), 88.

12 Eugen Dühring, *Die Judenfrage als Frage der Racenschädlichkeit für Existenz, Sitte und Cultur der Völker*, 4th ed. (Berlin: H. Reuther, 1892), 122–3.

13 Eugen Dühring, *Die Judenfrage als Frage des Rassencharakters und seiner Schädlichkiten für Eistenz und Kultur der Völker*, 6th ed. (Leipzig: O.R. Reisland, 1930), 127–8.

14 For Rosenberg's and Hitler's views on Zionism, see Francis Nicosia, *The Third Reich and the Palestine Question* (Austin: University of Texas Press, 1985), 20–8; and Robert Wistrich, 'Swastika, Crescent and Star of David,' in Robert Wistrich, ed., *Hitler's Apocalypse: Jews and the Nazi Legacy* (London: Weidenfeld and Nicolson, 1985), 154–63. The citation from *Mein Kampf* is reproduced in Wistrich, 155.

15 Cited by Marvin Kurz, 'Ernst Zundel Is More Dangerous Than You Realize,' *Globe and Mail*, 26 February 2003, A15.

16 On the history of the *Protocols* see Norman Cohn, *Warrant for Genocide: The Myth of the Jewish World Conspiracy and the Protocols of the Elders of Zion* (New York:

Harper and Row, 1967); Binjamin Segel, *A Lie and a Libel: The History of the Protocols of the Elders of Zion* (Lincoln, NE: University of Nebraska Press, 1995); and Erich Bronner, *A Rumor about the Jews: Reflections on Antisemitism and the Protocols of the Elders of Zion* (New York: St Martin's Press, 2000).

17 Thanks to Steven Zipperstein for this observation.

18 Cohn, *Warrant for Genocide*, 108. See also Segel, *A Lie and a Libel*, 71–9.

19 See the excerpts in Richard S. Levy, ed., *Antisemitism in the Modern World: An Anthology of Texts* (Lexington, MA: D.C. Heath, 1991), 169–77.

20 Mark R. Cohen, *Under Crescent and Cross: The Jews in the Middle Ages* (Princeton, NJ: Princeton University Press, 1994), 3–14.

21 Ron Nettler, 'Islamic Archetypes of the Jews: Then and Now,' in Robert Wistrich, ed., *Anti-Zionism and Antisemitism in the Contemporary World* (London: Macmillan, 1990), 63–73.

22 Cohen, *Under Crescent and Cross*, 167.

23 Yehoshua Porath, 'Anti-Zionist and Anti-Jewish Ideology in the Arab Nationalist Movement in Palestine,' in Almog, *Antisemitism through the Ages*, 217–26.

24 Muhhamad Muslih, *The Origins of Palestinian Nationalism* (New York: Columbia University Press, 1988), 75, 77–8. Citation is from 78.

25 Elyakim Rubinstein, '"Ha-protokolim shel ziknei tsiyon" ba-sikhsukh ha-'aravi-yehudi be-eretz yisra'el bi-shenot ha-'esrim,' *Ha-mizrah he-hadash* 26 (1976): 37–42.

26 Porath, 'Anti-Zionist and Anti-Jewish Ideology,' 223.

27 Muslih, *Origins of Palestinian Nationalism*, 169.

28 Constantine Zurayk, *The Meaning of the Disaster* (Beirut: Khayat's College Book Co-operative, 1956), 2.

29 Paul Berman, *Terror and Liberalism* (New York: Norton, 2003), 85–6.

30 Emmanuel Sivan, 'Islamic Fundamentalism, Antisemitism, and Anti-Zionism,' in Wistrich, *Anti-Zionism and Antisemitism in the Modern World*, 82.

31 Harkabi, 'On Arab Antisemitism Once More,' 238.

Chapter 7

The Nature and Determinants of Arab Attitudes towards Israel

MARK TESSLER

Antisemitism found its voice in Christian Europe when Jews were a diasporic and stateless community. Muslim communities, with some important exceptions, generally did not share in the traditional iconography of Christian antisemitism. The creation of the modern State of Israel altered the communitarian basis between Muslims and Jews and introduced an explicitly political dimension into their relationship. A Jewish state in the heartland of the Muslim world changed the political equation, but did the new politics spill over into a new antisemitism? In this essay, Mark Tessler carefully explores contemporary Arab attitudes towards Israel and argues that, although anti-Israel sentiment does sometimes express itself in anti-Jewish stereotypes, attitudes are largely shaped by the political relationship and change as the context changes. Nor is hostility to Israel a function of identification with Islam. Arab attitudes, he concludes, are politically determined rather than the consequence of an enduring impulse shaped by religion or culture.

* * *

Arab attitudes towards Israel are of interest for several reasons. On the one hand, in the context of the present volume, there is interest in determining the degree to which views about Israel are determined by views about Jews. More specifically, to what extent, if any, does antisemitism shape the way that many Arabs think about the Jewish state? On the other, beyond incorporating the Arab world into a broad assessment of antisemitism, a concern for Arab-Israeli peace makes it necessary to ask whether the Arabs, and especially ordinary citizens in the Arab world, are prepared to recognize Israel's right to exist and make peace with the Jewish state.

A review of Arab-Jewish relations unrelated to Israel is beyond the scope of the present essay. It may simply be noted, first, that it is difficult to offer generalizations about Jewish communities in the Arab world that apply across countries and time periods; and second, to the extent that a generalization may nonetheless be offered, it would be that Jews in the Arab world for the most part enjoyed physical security, communal autonomy, and opportunities for personal advancement. This is not to argue that antisemitism was totally absent or to deny that there were occasional, albeit infrequent, instances of anti-Jewish violence. It is rather to say that Arab attitudes towards Israel are not built on a foundation of intense and widespread anti-Jewish sentiment or on a legacy of persistent hostility towards the hundreds of thousands of Jews who lived in the Arab world prior to 1948.

In the years following Israeli independence, Arab opposition to the Jewish state did at least sometimes express itself in antisemitic terms. A disturbing example is to be found in the report of a September 1968 conference held at al-Azhar, the famous Islamic university in Cairo. The conference was organized by the Academy of Islamic Research and devoted to consideration of the Arab-Israeli conflict from a spiritual and theological perspective.[1] Further, some Israeli analysts and supporters of Israel asserted during this period that Arab refusal to recognize the Jewish state was motivated not by political consider-ations but rather by antisemitism. However, these accounts are often exagger-ated and propagandistic; they tend to ignore the Arabs' sincere conviction that Israel took land belonging to the Palestinians and instead allege, as one author wrote, that Arabs believe 'Israel and its people – indeed the Jewish people as a whole – are by their very nature evil ... [and that] Arab demonology probably goes even further than the worst excesses of the German Nazis ...'[2]

Some early accounts of Arab attitudes are more scholarly and credible. Particularly notable is that of Yehoshafat Harkabi, a prominent Israeli military intelligence analyst whose *Arab Attitudes to Israel* is based on a reading of original sources from the 1950s and 1960s.[3] Much of Harkabi's study, more frequently cited than actually read, shows Arab concern with justice for the Palestinians and security worries stemming from a fear of Israeli expansion. Moreover, by the 1980s Harkabi had come to believe that the Arab world was genuinely desirous of peace with Israel and that the territorial maximalism of the Israeli government was the most important obstacle to resolving the con-flict.[4] Nevertheless, Harkabi's early work also demonstrates that Arab anti-Zionist rhetoric did sometimes vilify Jews and spill over into antisemitism.

Against this background, the discussion to follow explores the nature and determinants of present-day Arab attitudes towards Israel. It draws upon a growing body of public opinion research and concludes that antisemitism is not a major factor in shaping Arab views, that considerations of political economy have a much greater influence on relevant attitudes than do culture and religion, and that there is broad support among Arabs, and especially among Palestinians, for a resolution of the Arab-Israeli conflict based on territorial compromise, mutual Israeli-Palestinian recognition, and reconciliation and normal interstate relations.

Anti-Israel Sentiment in the Arab World

Anti-Israel sentiment was strong and widespread in the Arab world during late 2002 and early 2003, in the run-up to the U.S.-led war against Saddam Hussein and the Baath regime in Baghdad. Moreover, anti-Israel sentiment had by this time been growing for several years, most especially since the eruption of the al-Aqsa intifada in September 2000. An indication of the depth and breadth of negative attitudes about Israel may be seen in the results of surveys carried out by Zogby International in March 2002.[5] Findings from Egypt, Jordan, Saudi Arabia, Kuwait, and Lebanon are shown in Figure 7.1. For purposes of parsimony, response distributions have been collapsed into three categories: very or somewhat favourable, unsure or somewhat unfavourable, very unfavourable. The figure shows that the proportion of those with very unfavourable attitudes towards Israel ranges from 79 per cent in Egypt to 97 per cent in Saudi Arabia.

The Zogby polls are not completely representative. They significantly over-represent educated and middle-class individuals and those who live in major cities. In the Egyptian survey, for example, 40 per cent of the respondents have had a college education and another 15 per cent have done postgraduate studies. This needs to be taken into consideration when drawing conclusions from the Zogby data. At the same time, attitudes towards Israel among less well-educated individuals are only somewhat less unfavourable, suggesting that a better sample might not produce very different results. Figure 7.2 shows the proportion of respondents with very unfavourable attitudes towards Israel among Egyptians with varying levels of education.

There is also evidence that anti-Israel sentiment sometimes expresses itself in anti-Jewish terms. For example, a post-9/11 opinion survey carried out in Egypt reported that approximately 90 per cent of those interviewed would not wish to have a Jewish neighbour. The survey, based on a nineteen-page questionnaire administered to a representative sample of 3,000 Egyptians over the age of fifteen, examined a wide range of social and political attitudes. It was supported by the U.S. National Science Foundation and carried out by Professor Mansoor Moaddel of Eastern Michigan University.[6]

There are two interrelated questions to be asked about the attitudes reflected

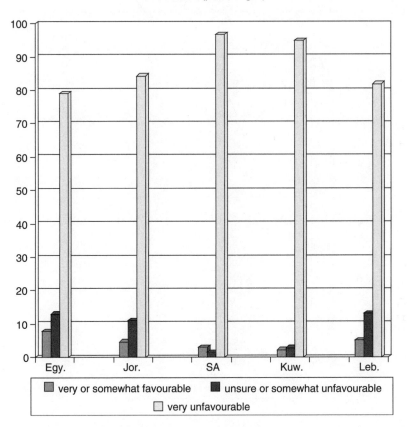

Figure 7.1. Attitudes towards Israel among Respondents Surveyed by Zogby International in March 2002 in Egypt, Jordan, Saudi Arabia, Kuwait, and Lebanon (percentages)

in these surveys: whether they are enduring or vary in accordance with events; and whether they indicate opposition to Israel's right to exist or to Israeli government policy. The data with which to address these questions are limited, making it impossible to advance definitive conclusions about the views held by ordinary Arab citizens. At the same time, as will be discussed more fully in the next section, available evidence strongly suggests that Arab attitudes towards Israel are highly sensitive to context, meaning that they are not primordial, do not reflect an enduring and unwavering opposition to Israel's existence, and are shaped in substantial measure by judgments about the nature and consequences of Israeli behaviour.

Figure 7.2. Proportion of Respondents with Very Unfavourable Attitudes towards Israel among Egyptians Surveyed by Zogby International in March 2002 and Classified According to Level of Education (percentages)

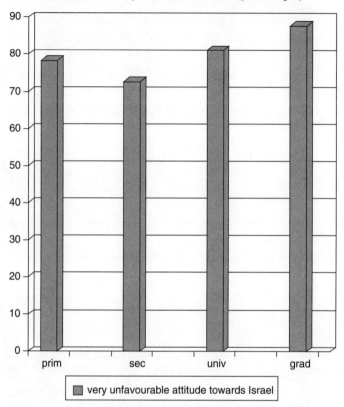

very unfavourable attitude towards Israel

It should be noted in this connection that the anger presently in evidence in the Arab world does not involve antipathy towards Israel alone. Attitudes towards the United States are only slightly less unfavourable. Yet, lest it be thought that this reflects some sort of fundamentalist anti-Western impulse, perhaps fostered by Islam, an analysis of data from a number of recent surveys leads to a rather different conclusion. First, unfavourable attitudes towards the United States are not mirrored in attitudes about France and Germany. Second, attitudes towards the United States are highly unfavourable only when respondents are asked about U.S. foreign policy; attitudes towards American education, American science, American democracy, and the American people are much

Figure 7.3. Percentage Holding Favourable Opinions of the United States, George W. Bush, and American Values among Jordanians Interviewed in 2002 and Grouped According to Age

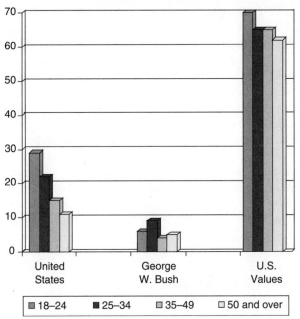

more favourable. Third, these more positive attitudes towards aspects of American society and culture are most pronounced among the younger generation and no less pronounced among individuals with strong religious attachments.

These findings are discussed in detail in two recent publications by the present author, one appearing in the United States and the other in the Arab world.[7] They are illustrated by the patterns shown in Figure 7.3, which presents findings from a highly representative survey carried out in Jordan in May and June 2002. The figure shows attitudes towards the United States, towards George W. Bush, and towards American values, and in each case it compares the views of respondents categorized by age. Attitudes towards the American values are generally quite positive, while attitudes towards the American president are almost never positive. Furthermore, attitudes towards the United States and towards American values are most positive among younger individuals and least positive among older individuals.

Making a connection between attitudes towards Israel and attitudes towards the United States requires an appreciation of the way that many in the Arab world view the political and economic status quo in their region. To begin, many see a region in which masses of people live in impoverished conditions and in which, for much of the population, especially the young, the prospects for social mobility and a higher standard of living are declining rather than growing brighter. Making matters worse, many also see a large and growing gap between rich and poor, and they accordingly complain that the burdens of underdevelopment are not shared equitably and that, despite widespread poverty, there are islands of affluence, often involving luxury and excess. Complaints about corruption and undeserved privilege may be noted as well. There is a widespread belief that elite membership is determined in most instances not by ability, dedication, or service to society but rather by personal and political connections, the result being a system where patronage and clientelism predominate in decisions about public policy and resource allocation.

There are few legitimate mechanisms by which ordinary men and women can register complaints about this situation in a way that will have a meaningful impact, and none whatsoever by which they can remove senior political leaders whose performance is judged unsatisfactory. In most Arab countries, expressions of discontent are tolerated, if at all, only to the extent that they do not threaten the established political and economic order, it being common for the state to suppress more serious forms of dissent.

Evidence that this view of the status quo is widespread, at least in such relatively poor Arab countries as Egypt, Jordan, Algeria, Morocco, Yemen, Tunisia, Syria, and the Palestinian Territories, which together contain roughly three-quarters of the Arab world's population, comes both from occasional opinion polls and from the analyses of Arab intellectuals. For example, a survey in Algeria in 1995–6 found that only 15 per cent of the 1,000 respondents interviewed believe that the government usually cares about the needs of ordinary citizens;[8] a 1997 survey in Egypt reported that 31 per cent judged their economic future to be insecure, with the percentage almost doubling among residents of Cairo;[9] a survey in Jordan in 1998 found that 68 per cent fear speaking out on political affairs, and only 16 per cent feel comfortable criticizing the government;[10] and a poll of West Bank and Gaza Palestinians in 2001 found that 71 per cent consider the Arafat regime to have a bad or very bad record on human rights and corruption.[11] Thus, according to a Jordanian journalist writing in 2000, 'a leading source of instability and political-economic distortion in the Arab world is the unchecked use of state power, combined with the state's whimsical ability to use the rule of law for its own political ends.'[12] There are numerous other articles and pronouncements in which Arab intellectuals make the same point.[13]

The relevance of all this to attitudes about the United States and Israel lies in a belief held by many that there is an alliance of domestic, regional, and international forces that works to maintain the status quo in the Middle East. This includes the United States, which has close ties to a number of undemocratic Arab regimes. And it includes Israel, which is closely allied with the United States and to which the United States is perceived to give excessive and uncritical support. Indeed, many Arabs believe that American policy towards Arab governments is driven largely by calculations about what is good for Israel. Accordingly, to the extent that large numbers of ordinary Arab citizens are discontented with the prevailing political and economic order, they ask about the power structure that supports the status quo, and they include the United States and Israel, along with their own governments, among the forces whose actions are inimical to their own welfare.

This analysis helps to explain why there was broad opposition in the Arab world to the U.S.-led war against the regime of Saddam Hussein that began in March 2003. While there was little love for Saddam, few trusted American motives or believed their circumstances would be better if the United States were victorious. This analysis also helps to explain why anger at the United States is accompanied by denunciations of Israel – why, for example, Israeli as well as American flags were burned when 200,000 Moroccans demonstrated in the capital, Rabat, against 'imperialist aggression' by the Anglo-American coalition.[14] The fact that Morocco is far from the Israeli-Palestinian conflict and has traditionally been in the forefront of efforts to promote peace between Israel and the Arabs makes this all the more significant.[15]

A recent op-ed article by *New York Times* columnist Tom Friedman offers a similar assessment of the basis for Arab anger and distrust of the United States. Writing in early April 2003, while American forces were still fighting their way to Baghdad, Friedman, too, emphasized both the status quo orientation of U.S. Middle East policy and the place of Israel in American strategic thinking about the region:

> Even after the cold war ended and America supported, and celebrated, the flowering of democracy from Eastern Europe to Latin America, the Arab world was excluded. In this neighbourhood, because of America's desire for steady oil supplies and a safe Israel, America continued to support the status quo and any Arab government that preserved it.[16]

Those who wish to consider this thesis further are directed to accounts of the Gulf Crisis of 1990–1, brought on by the Iraqi invasion and occupation of Kuwait.[17] Some Western observers were puzzled by the opposition of many in the Arab world to the U.S.-led campaign to remove Iraqi forces and restore the Kuwaiti monarchy. After all, Saddam had attacked a fellow Arab country. Further, he was a brutal dictator, and few would wish to live under his regime; he had been a willing client of the Soviet Union, and later to some extent the United States, so he hardly represented freedom from foreign influence; and he had gone to war with Iran to check the spread of Islamic influences, making him no champion of the religion. Finally, and significantly, the U.S.-led coalition included many Arab governments. Yet there were demonstrations against this coalition in many Arab countries, and again Israel, as well as America and Britain, was vehemently denounced. The reason, as summarized in an insightful study carried out at the time by a Moroccan sociologist, is that in the judgment of ordinary citizens the anti-Iraq coalition was composed of 'enemies of the people,' including 'bad Arab [governments whose] sole motivation ... was to remain in power and protect their personal interests ... to defend themselves against their own people, whom they fear.'[18]

There may be room for debate about whether the nature and motivations of U.S. Middle East policy are properly understood, and about whether American support for Israel is indeed uncritical and among the reasons the United States works to maintain the status quo in the Middle East. But to the extent that many in the Arab world believe this to be the case, it follows both that attitudes towards the United States are shaped by perceptions of U.S. policy and not an underlying 'clash of civilizations,' and that anger at Israel is driven to a significant degree by perceptions of Israeli policy and its influence on the United States, rather than by a more fundamental rejection of Israel's right to exist.

Determinants of Arab Attitudes towards Israel

The argument of the preceding section is that Arab attitudes towards Israel are for the most part shaped by contextual considerations and instrumental assessments, not by some deep and immutable opposition to Israel's existence. A more fundamental kind of rejection undoubtedly does characterize the views of some Arabs, including some intellectuals and some ordinary citizens. But this appears to be a minority opinion, both at the grass-roots level and among Arab leaders. More common is acceptance of a two-state solution based on territorial compromise and mutual Israeli-Palestinian recognition. Many have doubts that Israel would ever agree to such an accommodation, and these doubts are reinforced by a doubling of the number of Jewish settlers in the West Bank and Gaza since Israel and the PLO signed a Declaration of Principles in September 1993. Many thus complain that Israel values territorial expansion over peace with its neighbours, leading it to support a regional status quo that is inimical to the interests of most Arabs. But these complaints, whatever their validity and the intensity with which they are expressed, are about the nature and consequences of Israel's behaviour, not about Israel's existence.

Support for this assessment comes from the reception that Israel received in many Arab states following the Israel-PLO accord of 1993. It also comes from the many public opinion surveys carried out among Palestinians in the West Bank and Gaza and, though fewer in number, in several Arab states.

In signing the Declaration of Principles and agreeing to participate in a peace process that presumably would involve withdrawal from the West Bank and Gaza, Israel expected, and had a right to expect, that it would be accepted by the Arab world and have normal relations with Arab states. And despite rejectionism in some quarters, this occurred to a degree that was revolutionary. Many would add that there had long been indications of Arab readiness for peace with Israel. They cite the 1977 peace initiative of Anwar Sadat of Egypt, arguing that it was the Israeli government's refusal to consider withdrawal from the West Bank and Gaza that prevented other Arab states from following Egypt's lead. They also cite the Saudi peace initiative of 1981, as well as others, some dating back to the 1950s.[19] But while some supporters of Israel will argue that these early initiatives were neither serious nor sincere, apart from that of Sadat, few will disagree that there was a sea change following the 1993 accord. Once there was an agreement with provisions for Palestinian statehood and endorsed by the PLO, the sole legitimate representative of the Palestinian people, leaders and elites in a growing number of Arab countries concluded that there was no longer any reason to oppose peace with Israel. The Arab case against Israel, in other words, was based on the dispossession and statelessness of the Palestinians. With the establishment of a Palestinian state, in a part of historic Palestine and under terms agreed to by the PLO, there was no longer a basis for opposition.

Unprecedented Arab-Israel contact and cooperation blossomed on an individual, bilateral, and multilateral basis in the wake of the 1993 accord. In Jerusalem and Tel Aviv, in Arab capitals, and in Europe, Arab and Israeli businessmen and others met to discuss a wide range of joint ventures and other collaborations. A sense of the new momentum and its revolutionary character is given in the following excerpt from an *International Herald Tribune* article, written only eight months after the Israel-PLO accord was signed. The article is entitled 'When Former Enemies Turn Business Partners.'

Israel's transition from pariah to potential partner is most evident in the overtures to Israel by Arab governments and businessmen seeking potentially lucrative deals. Since September, Israeli officials have received VIP treatment in Qatar,

Oman, Tunisia, and Morocco. Qatar is studying how to supply Israel with natural gas. Egypt has launched discussions on a joint oil refinery, and officials talk of eventually linking Arab and Israeli electricity grids ... Millionaire businessmen from Saudi Arabia, Kuwait, Qatar and Bahrain [are] jetting off to London, Paris, and Cairo to meet Israelis, while Jordanians, Egyptians and Lebanese are rushing to Jerusalem for similar contacts.[20]

This account gives a feel for the expanding network of Arab-Israeli contacts and relationships after September 1993. Other examples include Israeli assistance to Oman on drip irrigation and desalination, the signing of an Israeli-Jordanian peace treaty, the opening of an Israeli 'Bureau de Liaison' in Morocco, Israeli-Tunisian cooperation on tourism, and an Egyptian-Jordanian-Israeli plan, with Saudi support, to deal with pollution in the Gulf of Aqaba. Saudi Arabia and other Gulf Cooperation Council countries ended their secondary and tertiary boycott of Israel at this time, and Arab states ceased their practice of challenging Israeli credentials at the United Nations. It is also noteworthy that Saudi Arabia's highest theological authority, Sheikh Abdel-Aziz ibn Baaz, issued a fatwa in December 1994 affirming the right of Saudi rulers to pursue normal relations with Israel. He cited a verse from the Koran: 'If thy enemy moves towards peace, you shall too, placing your dependence on God.'[21]

Still another tangible expression of the new era in Arab-Israeli relations is the convening of a series of international conferences to promote development in the context of peace. On 30 October – 1 November 1994, King Hassan of Morocco hosted the first of these conferences in Casablanca, with the goal of further normalizing Arab-Israeli relations clearly understood by all. The conference was attended by representatives of sixty-one countries and by 1,114 business leaders. Its leaders issued a declaration stating that they were 'united behind the vision ... of a comprehensive peace and a new partnership of business and government dedicated to furthering peace between Arabs and Israelis.'[22] Follow-up conferences were held in Jordan in 1995 and Cairo in 1996.

Not all Arab states jumped on this bandwagon, and the heady optimism of this period may seem naive when viewed from the vantage point of 2003, with Israelis and Palestinians fighting one another in the West Bank and Gaza and the Israeli flag being burned in many Arab capitals. But the point that Arab attitudes towards Israel are contextual, with a strong instrumental dimension, should nonetheless be clear. During a period when it appeared that Israel and the Palestinians had agreed on a two-state solution and were prepared to end their century-old conflict, large and growing numbers of Arab leaders and elites concluded that they no longer had any reason to oppose peace and normal relations with Israel. On the contrary, many rushed to take advantage of what they regarded as an important opportunity to obtain benefits for themselves and their countries.

The analysis of public opinion data supports a similar conclusion with respect to the attitudes of ordinary citizens. The greatest amount of information, and the most reliable information, comes from polls conducted by Palestinian research centres in the West Bank and Gaza. The Palestine Centre for Research and Studies, recently reorganized as the Palestinian Centre for Policy and Survey Research, and the Jerusalem Media and Communications Centre are the most important, though not the only, Palestinian institutions carrying out systematic public opinion research. Between them, they have conducted hundreds of polls since September 1993. With excellent sampling procedures and a corps of trained interviewers, both of these centres, and to a lesser extent others as well, provide a wealth of data with which to gauge the attitudes of ordinary Palestinians in the West Bank and Gaza.

Data from the West Bank and Gaza are clear and consistent. Despite some minor fluctuation in response to particular events, roughly two-thirds to three-quarters of the respondents in representative national surveys support peace with Israel. The questions sometimes ask about peace in general, sometimes about the peace process, and sometimes about reconciliation, but the findings are strikingly consistent both over time and across surveys conducted by different research centres, all of which gives additional confidence in the results. A selection of these findings is shown in Figure 7.4, which presents the results of surveys conducted in 1995, 1998, 2001, and 2002.[23]

It should be added that support for the *principle* of peace and reconciliation does not mean that Palestinians necessarily have confidence in Israel or the peace process. From their perspective, the period following the 1993 Israel-PLO accord did not see a reduction or even a freezing of Israel's presence in the Occupied Territories. On the contrary, it appeared to many Palestinians that Israel was using the peace process to buy time to expand the number of Jewish settlers in the West Bank and Gaza (and East Jerusalem) and thus make it increasingly unlikely that the question of borders and other final status issues would be resolved in a way that gave them meaningful statehood. But while this disappointment and distrust are also reflected in the survey findings, this makes it all the more significant that support for peace and reconciliation remained high.

All of the studies on which Figure 7.4 is based carried out bivariate and multivariate analyses of the data. Thus, while the figure presents only univariate frequency distributions, in order to show general tendencies, the scholarly publications that report on these surveys also examine the correlates and determinants of Palestinian attitudes towards peace with Israel. Two general

Figure 7.4. Attitudes towards Peace with Israel among Palestinians in the West Bank and Gaza Surveyed in 1995, 1998, 2001, and 2002 (percentages)

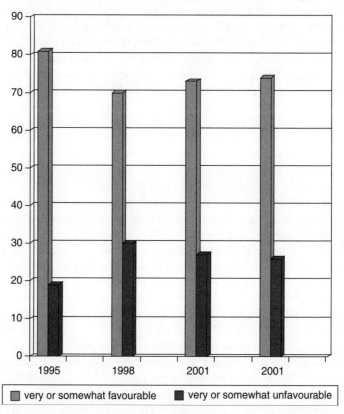

conclusions emerge from these more sophisticated analyses, both of which support the present essay's thesis about the importance of contextual factors and instrumental calculations.

First, orientations and attachments associated with Islam have at most only limited explanatory power; there is no empirical support for the proposition that Muslim Palestinians with a stronger attachment to or involvement in their religion are less likely than other Palestinians to have a favourable attitude towards Israeli-Palestinian peace and reconciliation. This is illustrated by the bivariate pattern shown in Figure 7.5, which compares the attitudes of more and less religious West Bank and Gaza Palestinians interviewed in 2001. The published analyses of the Palestinian data employ various survey questions and

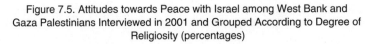

Figure 7.5. Attitudes towards Peace with Israel among West Bank and Gaza Palestinians Interviewed in 2001 and Grouped According to Degree of Religiosity (percentages)

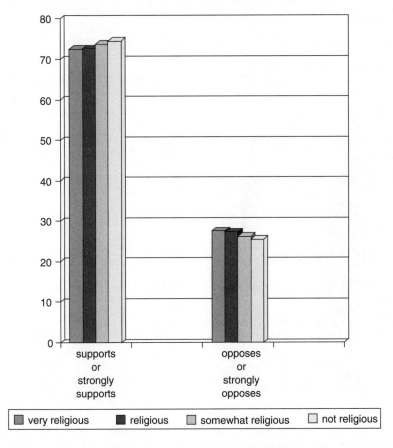

standard scaling techniques to measure religious orientations. They also employ multivariate statistical techniques in order to examine the relationship between attitudes towards peace and religious orientations with other factors held constant. In all cases, the findings are consistent with the pattern illustrated in Figure 7.5. Contrary to what is suggested by the 'clash of civilizations' thesis and similar assertions, at the individual level of analysis at least, Islam does not promote or encourage opposition to peace with Israel.

Relevant public opinion data from other Arab societies are rare. Systematic and rigorous political attitude research has been relatively scarce in the Arab

Figure 7.6. Attitudes towards Peace with Israel among Lebanese and Jordanians Surveyed in 1994 and Egyptians and Kuwaitis Surveyed in 1988 (percentages)

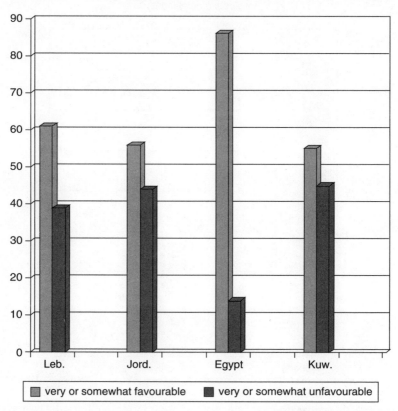

world, and this is particularly true of research that investigates attitudes towards Israel. But there are a few older studies that provide usable data, and findings from four of these are presented in Figure 7.6. They show that support for peace ranges from 85 per cent among Egyptians surveyed in 1988 to about 55 per cent for Jordanians and Kuwaitis interviewed in 1994 and 1988, respectively. Slightly above 60 per cent of the Lebanese respondents interviewed in 1994 also expressed support for peace. A more recent study carried out in Jordan in 2002 asked respondents whether or not they favoured strengthening Jordanian-Israeli relations and found that 27 per cent favoured this, 26 per cent preferred to keep relations at their present level, and 47 per cent wanted relations to be weakened.

These findings not only show that there is considerable variation with respect to attitudes about Israel, they also lend additional support to the view that opposition to peace is neither universal nor enduring. Moreover, and of particular relevance for the present discussion, in none of the surveys are attitudes affected by religious orientations. As with the Palestinian data, individuals who are more religious or otherwise have strong Islamic attachments are no less likely than others to be among those who favour peace with Israel.[24] Thus, again, it would be incorrect, at least at the individual level of analysis, to assume that Islam is an obstacle to Arab-Israeli peace.

The second general conclusion to emerge from a more sophisticated analysis of the survey data is that considerations of political economy, in contrast to considerations of religion and culture, do play an important role in shaping Arab attitudes towards Israel. This has been explored in detail with a number of different Palestinian data sets, and the results consistently show that attitudes towards economic well-being and towards political leadership are important influences on relevant political attitudes.[25]

To give but one illustration, Figure 7.7 shows that West Bank and Gaza Palestinians who believe that peace with Israel would bring economic benefits are more likely than others to favour reconciliation after a Palestinian state has been established. Figure 7.7 uses responses to a question about economic benefits for the respondent and his or her family, but the pattern is the same when using an item that asks about benefits for the Palestinian people in general. Judgments about the performance of the Palestinian Authority are similarly related to attitudes about reconciliation with Israel, and all of these political and economic assessments are also related in the same way to survey questions that ask about personal interaction with Israelis under conditions of peace. Each of these relationships is strong and statistically significant, and each remains so when examined with other factors held constant. Thus, again, it is clear that Palestinian and Arab attitudes towards Israel are neither unvarying nor uniformly hostile but, rather, are shaped in significant measure by contextual factors and instrumental considerations.

Other Dimensions of Arab Public Opinion

The Arab-Israeli conflict is not at the top of the political agenda of most people in the Arab world. This is not the case for Palestinians, of course, and Jordan is also a partial exception. But issues associated with governance and economic well-being are of much more immediate concern to the citizens of most Arab states. Indeed, as discussed earlier, views about Israel are heavily influenced by perceptions of its relationship to these more fundamental issues. More specifi-

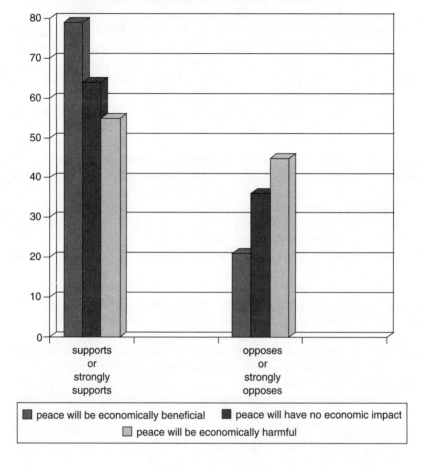

Figure 7.7. Attitudes towards Reconciliation with Israel among West Bank and Gaza Palestinians Interviewed in 2001 and Grouped According to Views about the Economic Consequences of Peace (percentages)

cally, there is discontent with the political and economic situation in many Arab states, anger at the United States for helping to perpetuate the status quo, and a belief that Israel plays a significant role in shaping U.S. Middle East policy.

Serious consideration of attitudes related to governance and political economy is beyond the scope of the present essay. But a brief discussion of attitudes about democracy may be useful in order to show that the role of context in shaping political orientations is not limited to views about Israel. For reasons that should be evident given the preceding discussion, support for accountable government, and hence for the most basic element of democratic governance, is widespread in the Arab world. This is illustrated by recent surveys in Egypt, Jordan, Algeria, and Morocco. In each case, a representative national survey carried out between 2000 and 2002 asked respondents whether or not they agreed that 'despite its problems, democracy is better than any other form of government.' In Egypt, only 2 per cent disagreed with this statement, whereas 34 per cent agreed and 64 per cent agreed strongly. Attitudes were even more positive in Morocco and only slightly less so in Jordan and Algeria.[26] Another study, using different data from Egypt, Algeria, and Morocco, as well as Palestine, reports slightly lower figures, in part because the interview schedule asked somewhat different questions about democracy.[27] But this research, too, shows that attitudes are skewed in favour of democratic governance.

Equally important and of particular relevance to the present discussion, attitudes towards democracy and governance, as with attitudes towards Israel, are relatively unaffected by religious orientations and are heavily influenced by political and economic factors. Several of these patterns are illustrated in Figures 7.8 and 7.9. Figure 7.8 shows the relationship between personal religiosity and attitudes towards democracy among a sample of 2,756 Egyptians interviewed in 2000. Attitudes towards democracy are measured by a composite index based on several questions from the interview schedule. The figure shows, again, that responses are heavily skewed in favour of democracy and that this is the case among more religious as well as less religious individuals. Thus, in contrast to the stereotypes common in Western countries, the religious attachments of ordinary Muslims do not predispose these men and women to regard democracy as an alien form of government with no relevance to their own societies. The most important reasons for the absence of democracy in much of the Arab world are not, therefore, to be found in the political culture of the 'Arab street.'[28]

Figure 7.9 presents a relationship that may be even more surprising to those with little knowledge of Arab and Muslim society. Using data from a representative sample of 2,264 Moroccans, it shows the relationship between support for democracy and attitudes towards political Islam. Questions about political Islam ask respondents whether they think religion should be an important source of guidance in political affairs, whether men of religious learning should play a major role in the governing of society, and so forth. In all of the countries where these questions were asked, there was a fairly even distribution of responses. In the Moroccan case, for example, one item asked whether it would be better for the country if more people with strong religious beliefs held public office. Thirty-one per cent agreed strongly, whereas 28 per cent disagreed or disagreed strongly. The remainder were divided almost equally between those

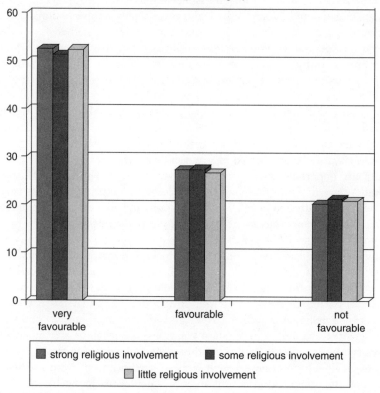

Figure 7.8. Attitudes towards Democracy among Egyptians Interviewed in 2000 and Grouped According to Degree of Involvement in Religious Activities and Practices (percentages)

who were neutral and those who agreed. In Egypt, only 13 per cent disagreed or disagreed strongly with this proposition, indicating greater support for political Islam. In Algeria and Jordan, by contrast, the numbers were 47 per cent and 32 per cent, respectively.

The most important point, however, as illustrated by Figure 7.9, is that a belief that there should be an important connection between religion and politics does not imply a preference for an authoritarian form of government. Rather, those with a positive attitude towards political Islam are just as well represented among the many individuals who support democracy as are those who favour a separation of religion and politics. This says something important about how ordinary citizens in the Arab world think about Islam. It also

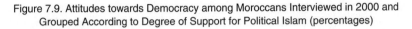

Figure 7.9. Attitudes towards Democracy among Moroccans Interviewed in 2000 and Grouped According to Degree of Support for Political Islam (percentages)

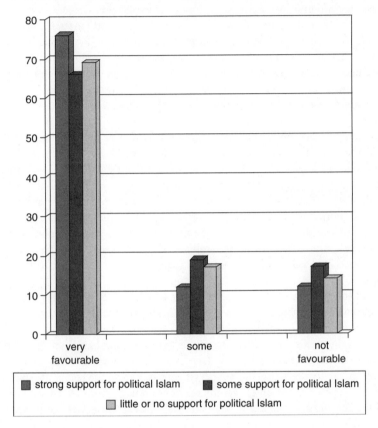

provides additional evidence that Arab attitudes are not shaped by some sort of religion-based clash of civilizations that breeds hostility towards the United States, Western institutions, and Israel.

This discussion of the degree and determinants of support for democracy could be amplified considerably. Further attention to the nature and determinants of attitudes towards political Islam would also be instructive. Attitudes about women and gender equality is yet another area where misconceptions about Arabs and Muslims are common in the West. Readers wishing to explore these subjects will be well rewarded, and for the most part they will find once again both that views are more diverse and nuanced than they might have assumed and that contextual considerations and rational calculations play a critical role in determining what people think. In other words, Arabs and Muslims form opinions in the same way as everyone else.

This is not to deny that there are some ideologues and fanatics in the Arab world. No society, including the United States and including Israel, is totally free of such individuals. These people see the world through the prism of a particular mind set, very possibly one derived from their conception of religious obligation. They may also believe that any and all means are justified to achieve the ends defined by their morality. But this is not the way most ordinary citizens think, and it is no more appropriate to try to understand the true character of Islam by looking at Osama bin Laden or other fanatics than it would be to say the true essence of Judaism is defined by Meir Kahane, Baruch Goldstein, or Yigal Amir. And if there is sometimes support and sympathy for such men among ordinary citizens, as there was in 1991 for the secular Saddam Hussein, it is because people are desperate for change and see no credible alternative to deal with their grievances. Accordingly, while it is unrealistic to believe that any society can be purged of its fanatics completely, these individuals will be isolated and marginalized to the extent that grievances are recognized and other ways to address them are made available to ordinary citizens.

And so it is with Arab attitudes towards Israel. There is no doubt that anti-Israel sentiment is broad and deep in the Arab world at the present time. But this sentiment is not fuelled by primordial hatred or an enduring rejection of Israel's right to exist. Most Arabs continue to believe that Israel's creation did an injustice to the Palestinians. Many Israelis would acknowledge this as well. Yet many and almost certainly most Arab citizens recognize the reality of Israel and would accept, even welcome, peaceful relations under appropriate conditions.

One condition required for Arab acceptance of Israel is that the country be genuinely committed to an accommodation with the Palestinians based on territorial compromise and mutual recognition, as it appeared to be when it signed the Declaration of Principles in 1993. A second condition is that Israeli policies should not contribute to the perpetuation of a regional status quo that is detested by most ordinary men and women. The degree to which Israel meets these conditions will be determined in large measure by its own policies and actions. Some may also wish to argue that Arab perceptions are distorted and that the government in Jerusalem has already done more than its share to meet reasonable Arab demands. Making this argument will be difficult at the present time, given events in the West Bank and Gaza and support from pro-Israel quarters for the U.S.-led war in Iraq. But even if perceptions of Israel *are* distorted, it remains the case that Arab attitudes towards Israel are determined primarily by considerations of context and consequence, real or perceived, and not by any fundamental and enduring impulse shaped by religion, culture, or some other deep-seated normative orientation.

NOTES

1 D.F. Green, *Arab Theologians on Jews and Israel* (Geneva: Editions de l'Avenir, 1976). For accounts of Muslim scholars and jurists at al-Azhar later offering a different view, affirming that Egypt's 1979 peace treaty with Israel is not contrary to Islamic law, see Derek Hopwook, *Egypt: Politics and Society, 1945–1981* (London: Allen and Unwin, 1982), 119; and Johannes J.G. Jansen, *The Neglected Duty: The Creed of Sadat's Assassins and the Islamic Resurgence in the Middle East* (London: Macmillan, 1986), 44. Islam's attitude towards peace with Israel is also discussed in Mark Tessler and Marilyn Grobschmidt, 'Democracy in the Arab World and the Arab-Israeli Conflict,' in David Garnham and Mark Tessler, eds, *Democracy, War, and Peace in the Middle East* (Bloomington: Indiana University Press, 1995).

2 Samuel Katz, *Battleground: Fact and Fantasy in Palestine* (New York: Bantam Books, 1973), 175.

3 Yehoshafat Harkabi, *Arab Attitudes to Israel* (Jerusalem: Israel Universities Press, 1970). See also Yehoshafat Harkabi, 'The Arab Ideology of the Conflict,' in Gil Carl Alroy, eds, *Attitudes toward Jewish Statehood in the Arab World* (New York: American Academic Association for Peace in the Middle East, 1971).

4 Yehoshafat Harkabi, *Israel's Fateful Hour* (New York: Harper Collins, 1989).

5 'Arab Nations' "Impressions of America" Poll' (Utica, NY: Zogby International, 2002).

6 Mansoor Moaddel, 'Public Opinion in Islamic Countries: Survey Results,' *Footnotes* 31 (January 2003). *Footnotes* is published by the American Sociological Association. This report presents only a few of the research findings; more detailed analyses are in preparation.

7 Mark Tessler and Dan Corstange, 'How Should Americans Understand Arab and Muslim Political Attitudes: Combating Stereotypes with Public Opinion Data from the Middle East,' *Journal of Social Affairs* 19 (Winter 2002): 13–24. Mark Tessler, 'Arab and Muslim Political Attitudes: Stereotypes and Evidence from Survey Research,' *International Studies Perspectives* 4 (May 2003): 175–80.

8 Mark Tessler, 'Islam and Democracy in the Arab World: Evidence from Opinion Research in the Maghrib,' in Amin Saikal and Albrecht Schnabel, eds, *Democracy and Peace in the Middle East* (Tokyo: United Nations University, 2003).

9 Nevine Khalil, 'Listening to the Masses' [Arabic], *Al-Ahram Weekly*, 1–7 October 1998.

10 Emmanuel Sivan, 'Illusions of Change,' *Journal of Democracy* 11 (2000): 69–83.

11 Jodi Nachtwey and Mark Tessler, 'The Political Economy of Attitudes toward Peace among Palestinians and Israelis,' *Journal of Conflict Resolution* 46 (2) (April 2002): 260–85.

12 Rami Khouri, 'A View from the Arab World,' *Jordan Times*, 5 July 2000. See also Rami Khouri, 'Politics and Perceptions in the Middle East after September 11,' *Social Science Research Council*, 'Contemporary Conflicts' website: http://conconflicts.ssrc.org/mideast/.

13 See, for example, Mohamed Talbi, 'A Record of Failure,' *Journal of Democracy* 11 (2000): 58–68.

14 Associated Press, 30 March 2003.

15 Mark Tessler, 'Moroccan-Israeli Relations and the Reasons for Moroccan Receptivity to Contact with Israel,' *Jerusalem Journal of International Relations* 10 (Spring 1988): 76–108.

16 Thomas Friedman, 'Come the Revolution,' *New York Times*, 2 April 2003.

17 Mark Tessler, 'Anger and Governance in the Arab World: Lessons from the Maghrib and Implications for the West,' *Jerusalem Journal of International Relations* 13 (Fall 1991): 7–33; David Pollock, *The 'Arab Street'? Public Opinion in the Arab World* (Washington: Washington Institute for Near East Policy, Policy Paper No. 32, 1992); Abdelkader Zghal, 'La Guerre du Golfe et la recherche de la bonne distance,' in *La Guerre du Golfe et l'avenir des Arabes: Débats et réflexions* (Tunis: Cérès Productions, 1991).

18 Mounia Bennani-Chraibi, *Soumis et rebelles: Les jeunes au Maroc* (Paris: CNRS Editions, 1994), 243.

19 See Mark Tessler, *A History of the Israeli-Palestinian Conflict* (Bloomington: Indiana University Press, 1994), 338–41. See also Itamar Rabinovich, *The Road Not Taken: Early Arab-Israeli Negotiations* (Oxford: Oxford University Press, 1991), 199–200.

20 Caryle Murphy and Nora Boustany, 'When Former Enemies Turn Business Partners,' *International Herald Tribune*, 24 May 1994. See also Peter Waldman, 'Guns and Butter: Khashoggi Is Back, Angling for a Profit from Middle East Peace,' *Wall Street Journal*, 4 February 1994. For a fuller discussion, see Mark Tessler, 'Israel at Peace with the Arab World,' *Occasional Papers of the Emirates Center for Strategic Studies and Research* (Abu Dhabi: Emirates Center for Strategic Studies and Research, 1995), 7–37.

21 Youssef Ibrahim, 'Muslims Argue Theology of Peace with Israel,' *New York Times*, 31 January 1995.

22 'Middle East/North Africa Economic Summit: Casablanca Declaration,' distributed by the Israeli Consulate Information Department, 2 November 1994.

23 Details about the studies on which Figure 7.4 is based, including sampling

methods, the interview schedule, and evidence of measurement reliability and validity, can be found in the following publications: Mark Tessler and Jodi Nachtwey, 'Islam and Attitudes toward International Conflict: Evidence from Survey Research in the Arab World,' *Journal of Conflict Resolution* 42 (October 1998): 619–36; Mark Tessler and Jodi Nachtwey, 'Palestinian Political Attitudes: An Analysis of Survey Data from the West Bank and Gaza,' *Israel Studies* 4 (Spring 1999):

22–43; Nachtwey and Tessler, 'The Political Economy of Attitudes toward Peace among Palestinians and Israelis'; Jacob Shamir and Khalil Shikaki, 'Determinants of Reconciliation and Compromise among Israelis and Palestinians,' *Journal of Peace Research* 39 (March 2002): 85–202; Khalil Shikaki, 'The Transition to Democracy in Palestine,' *Journal of Palestine Studies* 98 (Winter 1996): 2–14.

24 Tessler and Nachtwey, 'Islam and Attitudes toward International Conflict. See also Mark Tessler and Jamal Sanad, 'Will the Arab Public Accept Peace with Israel: Evidence from Surveys in Three Arab Societies,' in Gregory Mahler and Efriam Karsh, eds, *Israel at the Crossroads* (London: I.B. Tauris, 1994).

25 Nachtwey and Tessler, 'The Political Economy of Attitudes toward Peace among Palestinians and Israelis.'

26 Mark Tessler, 'Do Islamic Orientations Influence Attitudes toward Democracy in the Arab World: Evidence from Egypt, Jordan, Morocco, and Algeria,' *International Journal of Comparative Sociology* 2 (Spring 2003): 229–49.

27 Mark Tessler, 'Islam and Democracy in the Middle East: The Impact of Religious Orientations on Attitudes toward Democracy in Four Arab Countries,' *Comparative Politics* 34 (April 2002): 337–54.

28 In addition to the publications cited above, an extended discussion and additional references can be found in Mark Tessler, 'Democratic Concern and Islamic Resurgence: Converging Dimensions of the Arab World's Political Agenda,' in Howard Handelman and Mark Tessler, eds, *Democratization and Its Limits: Lessons from Latin American, Asia, and the Middle East* (Notre Dame: Notre Dame University Press, 1999).

Contributors

Todd M. Endelman is director of the Jean and Samuel Frankel Center for Judaic Studies and William Haber Professor of Modern Jewish History at the University of Michigan. His most recent book is *The Jews of Britain, 1656–2000* (University of California Press, 2002).

The Honourable R. Roy McMurtry has been Chief Justice of Ontario since 1996. He has served as chief justice and associate chief justice of the Ontario Superior Court of Justice, attorney general for Ontario, and Canadian ambassador to the United Kingdom.

The Right Honourable Brian Mulroney was Prime Minister of Canada between 1984 and 1993.

Derek J. Penslar is Zacks Professor of History and director of the Jewish Studies Program at the University of Toronto. His books include *Shylock's Children: Economics and Jewish Identity in Modern Europe* (2001). He is co-editor of *The Journal of Israeli History*.

Mark Tessler is Samuel J. Eldersveld Collegiate Professor of Political Science at the University of Michigan, where he is also vice-provost for international affairs and director of the university's International Institute. He has written extensively on Israel, the Arab world, and the Israeli-Palestinian conflict.

Morton Weinfeld is professor of sociology at McGill University, where he holds the chair in Canadian ethnic studies. He has published widely in the areas of ethnicity in general and Canadian Jewish life in particular. His most recent book is *Like Everyone Else, But Different: The Paradoxical Success of Canadian Jews* (McClelland and Stewart, 2001).

Steven J. Zipperstein is Daniel E. Koshland Professor in Jewish Culture and History and co-director of the Taube Center for Jewish Studies at Stanford University. His most recent book is *Imagining Russian Jewry: Memory, History, Identity* (University of Washington Press, 1999), and he is currently at work on a cultural history of East European and Russian Jewry from the eighteenth century to the present. He is co-editor of *Jewish Social Studies: History, Culture, and Society.*